THE LAWS OF
PROSPERITY

Building a Divine Foundation of Success

E. BERNARD JORDAN

ATRIA BOOKS
New York London Toronto Sydney New Delhi

BEYOND WORDS
Hillsboro, Oregon

ATRIA BOOKS
A Division of Simon & Schuster, Inc.
1230 Avenue of the Americas
New York, NY 10020

BEYOND WORDS
20827 N.W. Cornell Road, Suite 500
Hillsboro, Oregon 97124-9808
503-531-8700 / 503-531-8773 fax
www.beyondword.com

Managing editor: Lindsay S. Brown
Editor: Aaron D. Lewis
Copyeditor: Mark Antonides
Proofreader: Kristin Thiel
Design: Devon Smith
Composition: William H. Brunson Typography Services

First Atria Books/Beyond Words hardcover edition September 2011

ATRIA BOOKS and colophon are trademarks of Simon & Schuster, Inc.
Beyond Words Publishing is a division of Simon & Schuster, Inc.

For more information about special discounts for bulk purchases, please contact Simon & Schuster Special Sales at 1-866-506-1949 or business@simonandschuster.com.

The Simon & Schuster Speakers Bureau can bring authors to your live event. For more information or to book an event, contact the Simon & Schuster Speakers Bureau at 1-866-248-3049 or visit our website at www.simonspeakers.com.

Manufactured in the United States of America

10 9 8 7 6 5 4 3 2

Library of Congress Cataloging-in-Publication Data

Jordan, E. Bernard.
  The laws of prosperity : building a divine foundation of success / E. Bernard Jordan.
    p. cm.
  Includes index.
  1. Wealth—Religious aspects—Christianity.   I. Title.
  BR115.W4J669   2011
  241'.68—dc22

                                                    2011014131

ISBN: 978-1-58270-316-9
ISBN: 978-1-4516-3299-6 (ebook)

The corporate mission of Beyond Words Publishing, Inc.: *Inspire to Integrity*

This book is dedicated to my youngest child,
Prophet Yakim Manasseh Robert Jordan.
My prayer is that you understand and demonstrate
these dynamic spiritual and metaphysical principles
for your generation and help others to
reach for their greatness.

■ ■ ■ ■ ■

CONTENTS

∷ ∷ ∷ ∷ ∷

CONTENTS

Acknowledgments

TIM VANDEHEY, thank you for your angelic contributions to help give this book the "halo" effect that was needed to catapult these powerful spiritual and metaphysical principles into the atmosphere.

DR. AARON LEWIS, thank you for being my literary agent and for giving me a voice once again in the publishing industry.

PASTOR JE'NISE GOSS, thank you for serving as my on-staff copy editor and for your assistance in getting this book completed.

INTRODUCTION

■   ■   ■   ■   ■

The world is filled with grim news about the economy. As I was putting the finishing touches on this book, unemployment in the United States was hovering above 9.5 percent, its highest level in more than twenty-five years. More than nine million jobs had been lost since the economy hit its peak. More than three million home-owners were expected to go into foreclosure. Credit card defaults were at an all-time high. The litany of pain, confusion, loss, and poverty seemed endless.

The word *recession* means "the act of receding or withdrawing." In terms of the Divine economy, God is in recession because we as human beings have been receding, withdrawing, from the core principles that create not only temporal but spiritual wealth. In our haste to acquire material possessions for their own sake and to pursue more while sacrificing better, we let ourselves forget about the realities of self and Mind that brought wealth to us in the first place. We were blinded by greed and distracted by the promise of quick riches and the flash of the new, the seductive, and the temporary.

In *The Laws of Prosperity*, you will find, in addition to brilliant ideas from New Thought leaders such as John Shelby Spong and Marianne Williamson, thoughts from leaders of business and finance, from Steve Forbes to Alan Greenspan. These people represent the modern economy for better or worse, and we cannot ignore their wisdom (or lack of wisdom) as we come to understand not just how we can create greater, deeper prosperity for ourselves but how we can help steer our culture back toward an emphasis on the wealth of consciousness and away from shallow, empty pursuits of riches for their own sake.

You will leave these pages with the fundamental education you require to become an expert in financial thinking. Forget about financial planning; if your thinking isn't right, you won't have any money to plan or manage. You will develop a greater ability to:

- Recognize hubris
- Set aside greed
- Create security for yourself and your family
- Pull yourself out of a financial crisis
- Get and stay out of debt
- Reorient your values toward what makes you truly happy
- Establish a never-ending stream of Divine wealth flowing toward you
- Live more fully, happily, and generously
- Escape the cycle of boom and bust
- Build your own personal microeconomy based on the infinite power of Mind

The failure of our society, which led to the economic disasters that befell our culture, was born of *hubris*. The Bible says that "pride goeth before a fall," and hubris is a particularly dangerous breed of pride. In essence, it means "overbearing pride and arrogance that leads to self-destruction." Victor Frankenstein, of the novel *Frankenstein*, is a good example of hubris. The good doctor thought that he could defy the laws of God and nature and restore life to the dead, but he ended up creating a monster. We have done the same thing with the world's economy—created a monster—because we chose to ignore the essential laws of God's economy, which underlie the earthly economy. In doing so, we crafted a catastrophe out of equal parts avarice, self-indulgence, and self-delusion that the price paid would not have to match the thing gained. We allowed ourselves to drift away from the wisdom that drives the Divine economy, and we have seen the results.

GOD'S ECONOMIC POLICY

What cosmic economic laws did we ignore? The very laws that allowed the enlightened among us to tap into the true source of all abundance, the Mind. These are the mechanisms ordained by God to turn the wheels of the universal economic system:

1. Each of us is God pressed out into the physical world; we are agents of the Divine, each with a small aspect of the Divine purpose.

2. Each of us has a Mind that is embedded in the substance of the One-Mind and entangled with all other Minds.

3. Because all things, beings, and moments in time are part of the wholeness of God (who can also be thought of as Consciousness), God creates by becoming that which he wishes to manifest. As I explain in my book *Cosmic Economics*, when you begin to enter into higher consciousness, you begin to say, "I am that." It takes you beyond the surface understanding that "God is in the bird" or "God is in the elephant" or "God is in man." It goes deeper

than that. God *is* the bird. God *is* the elephant. God *is* the man. God *is* you—and this is what is known as "I Am."

4. We can create new wealth, people, or opportunity in the material world only by doing as God does, by stating *I Am* that which we intend to manifest. Intention does matter. Whatever the Mind focuses its attention on is what becomes our reality.

Those are the fundamental principles of operating within the Divine economy. We are creatures not of body, but of Mind, and we must follow the edicts of the Divine system if we are to materialize new businesses, homes, relationships, and health in our lives. We must understand that we are not the source of what comes to us; we are merely the conduits, and we must approach the universe with humility and self-awareness. Sadly, in recent years many of us have not done this. Instead, as we began to believe that we could experience infinite financial growth without consequences, we began to believe that we, not God, were the sources of our good fortune. The Bible says that we cannot serve both God and Mammon, so we chose Mammon. Mammon is the disproportionate affection for money that distorts our sense of reality. In placing Mammon above God, we began to follow a new set of false principles:

1. Humans are the essential source of wealth and prosperity.

2. We create wealth and abundance by manipulating markets and working endlessly. Our minds are merely tools to allow us to create new tools to manipulate markets.

3. Values such as thrift, moderation, generosity, and common sense are optional and easy to abandon.

4. We have no higher purpose beyond the continual gathering of more.

It is easy to see how adopting such empty, self-absorbed ideas could bring us down as individuals, along with the entire national and global economic systems. When we give up orienting our Minds on our desires and instead believe that we are sufficient to bring about changes to the fundamental nature of the world, we fail. Arrogant, self-important financial kings deluded themselves into thinking that "this time is different," that they could rewrite the economic laws. Some simply lied and cheated their way to ruin. Millions of people bought into the lies, setting aside their disciplined minds to grasp at wealth that seemed easy and available.

But we are not the source of our wealth or plenty. We have never been. God is the ultimate source, and his Divine nature grants us the power to order and manifest whatever kind of reality we can create. All new things—inventions, governments, works of art, even religious creeds—begin as ideas in a fertile Mind skilled at manifestation. We have only to hold the I Am in our minds, and gradually the forces of the universe pool and gather like an accumulating electrical current to break into the material plane and give us our desire. That is the nature of God's economy. But when we turn our backs on that truth, we betray everything God has given us. We betray ourselves and what Abraham Lincoln called "the better angels of our nature."

ABUNDANCE LIES WITHIN

Abundance and lack exist in the Mind before they exist in the physical world. When times are hard, you must first look within at how your Mind is shaping the world around you. Are you adhering to your core values and orienting your Mind on them at all times? If you are, then you will know it, because those values will become manifest. If a woman who defines wealth as fidelity and freedom from debt bases her entire being on those values, they will constantly come into her orbit. She will enjoy a faithful mate and debt will rarely stay around for long. But if she tosses away those fundamental values and lets her mind be drawn to the shallow, base pursuit of mere things, she will focus on what she does not have. That lack will infect her mind, and eventually it will become her reality.

No matter how we act, the Laws do not change; the Mind is always shaping the fabric of reality on the spiritual level. Spirit and Mind are of the same stuff. When you narrow the power of the mind with your intention and state I Am that which you desire, that power is creative. When you let thoughts of greed, anxiety, and envy run loose, they turn the Mind's power against you. Your wayward thinking becomes a self-fulfilling prophecy.

THE LAWS OF PROSPERITY

There is nothing inherently wrong with money. It is a tool to be used according to the spirit that possesses it. Money is God's power for change in the human world. Little changes without money, which is why organizations that fight hunger or try to find cures for disease always ask for money. Money moves people and brings ideas into being. It can be a holy thing. But many of us are seduced by Mammon, which can make us think we are masters of the universe and that we have it all figured out. It makes us ignore God, and worse, ignore the fact that we are God.

If you surrendered some of your core values to pursue the easy money or to chase the temporary high of acquisition, then you did bring some of your misfortune upon yourself. Happily, there is a path back to prosperity.

Discovering and acting on the Laws of Prosperity is the way to reorient your Mind, prevent future sliding into a valueless state, and enhance your own ability to create wealth and abundance for yourself and others. You will discover a new ability to transform your Mind to radiate abundance and health in concert with your dearest values. You will end your financial woes. You will redefine your earthly existence. You will find harmony with your true purpose. Abundance lies within each of us when it translates into values, action, consistency, and wisdom. In the hands of someone Divinely Enlightened, money is a positive force for fulfilling God's Plan.

Based on the teachings of the Bible, I suggest these as what we might consider the Laws of God, Economist.

The Law of Clarity—See today's situation as it truly is, rather than hiding in comfortable self-delusion.

The Law of Compensation—When one thing goes out of your life, another enters to compensate and maintain balance.

The Law of Debt—You cannot escape your obligations.

The Law of Discipline—If something appears to be an easy path to prosperity, it is probably false.

The Law of Divine Purpose—If God denies you wealth, it's because you were doing the wrong things with it.

The Law of Employment—Idleness is a waste of Divine energy.

The Law of Entanglement—Each of us is connected to, or entangled with, every other Mind in the cosmos. This can also be called the Law of One-Mind.

The Law of Fertility—You can till the soil of your economic future today with the right deeds and thoughts.

The Law of Hidden Patterns—Life is like the stock market: there are patterns underlying what appears to be chaos. You never know when the "bounce" is going to happen that will change your fortunes.

The Law of Humility—Being humble leads to the willingness to make wealth-creating changes.

The Law of Investment—Money begets money, and prosperous thought begets prosperous thought.

The Law of Mental Capital—You will gain when you allow other people to tap the power of your Mind for their benefit.

The Law of Obstacles—Failure is God's classroom. Attend class.

The Law of Parsimony—The simplest solution is the best one.

The Law of Quantum Abundance—Reality operates at the quantum level, in which all your opportunities already exist, waiting to be perceived by your Mind.

The Law of Recession—Sometimes, things in your life contract or pull away, but it is always for a good reason.

The Law of Rising Tide—What is good for everyone is also good for you.

The Law of Service—Assisting someone in economic need delivers assistance for you.

The Law of the Contract—If you want something specific in your experience, then you must create a contract with God and the Universe to achieve it.

The Law of Values—You must always be guided by core values that lock your mind on your desires.

Your Divine Stimulus Plan

As you learn and master these twenty laws, you will discover that they make up your personal Divine Stimulus Plan. Where the US president's financial stimulus plan was designed to spark spending and investment in the corporeal world, this spiritual stimulus is intended to spark activity in the true source of economic growth, your Mind. Discovering the potential of the laws and your ability to put them into action will stimulate you both to find the Divine spark of prosperity in yourself and to rediscover the essence of any personal values you may have set aside in the past few years because pursuing material wealth seemed more important. Let me tell you this: when you become wealthy in Spirit and Mind, your hands will overflow with material wealth!

> In hope, peace, and wealth,
> E. Bernard Jordan

I

THE LAW OF CLARITY

■ ■ ■ ■ ■

CORE PRINCIPLES

- The unenlightened Mind naturally seeks out that which comforts it, real or not.

- Self-delusion is the root of misfortune.

- Seeing the true situation clearly empowers us to take productive action and manifest change.

We are all weak, finite, simple human beings, standing in the need of prayer. None need it so much as those who think they are strong, those who know it not, but are deluded by self-sufficiency.

—Harold C. Phillips

In 2009, investment guru Bernard Madoff announced to the world that he was guilty of running the largest Ponzi scheme in the history of mankind and that his perfidy had cost his investors—many of whom were (normally) savvy, educated businesspeople and financial professionals—more than $50 billion. Because Madoff had simply used funds from later investors to repay earlier ones and absconded with much of the money himself, a staggering amount of wealth, including the life's savings of thousands of families, vaporized overnight.

Why was this possible? As Sheldon Filger, founder of Global EconomicCrisis.com, wrote, "Among the multitude of Madoff clients who were literally picked clean of their life savings, I was struck by the contradiction between their apparent intelligence and acute naiveté."[1] Madoff attracted new investors by walking and talking the part, schmoozing Wall Street and Securities and Exchange Commission officials to say glowing things about him and, most of all, by promising outrageous returns of up to 46 percent annually.

---

1. Sheldon Filger, "Bernie Madoff and the Art of Financial Self-Delusion," *Global Economic Crisis* (blog), July 1, 2009, http://www.globaleconomiccrisis.com/blog/archives/445.

To give you some perspective, the annual average for the stock market over the last fifty years has been 8 percent annually.

The attractive power of this ridiculous promise is instructive for us as we begin our journey into the Laws of Prosperity. Common sense teaches us, usually by the time we are in middle school, that we cannot get something for nothing. Cosmic balance dictates that an equal price must be paid for everything we acquire. You probably discovered this principle when you sent away for a pair of X-ray glasses advertised on the back of a comic book only to find that they didn't work, or when you ate an entire box of cereal to get the toy at the bottom and discovered to your disappointment that it was cheap plastic and broke in five minutes. As human beings, we seem to have a bottomless talent for deluding ourselves about what someone else can and is offering us (we see silver when it's really a ball of tinfoil); what we could have in that exact time and place (no matter intentions, perseverance, or skills, a person stranded on a desert island cannot eat a gourmet five-course meal that night); and most important and most difficult to self-detect, what we truly want.

It was this that allowed Madoff to wreak such havoc and destroy so many lives. Investors who should have known better flocked to his company because their greed overwhelmed their common sense. In fact they did know better. They engaged in the self-delusion— amid warnings from wiser people (including their mothers) that "if something seems too good to be true, it probably is"—believing it would be different for them this time. They wanted to feel smarter than other investors, part of an insiders' club. They wanted to reap the rewards—both money and superiority—of their wisdom. Sadly, many of them have reaped only poverty, with some former Madoff clients forced to forage for food in dumpsters.

SEE THINGS CLEARLY OR DON'T LOOK

The great Bishop John Shelby Spong wrote, "Integrity and honesty, not objectivity and certainty, are the highest virtues to which the theological enterprise can aspire. From this perspective, all human claims to possess objectivity, certainty, or infallibility are revealed as nothing but the weak and pitiable pleas of frantically insecure people who seek to live in an illusion because reality has proved to be too difficult."[2] That is the essence of the Law of Clarity.

THE LAW OF CLARITY

You must see yourself, the world around you, your situation, and your opportunities with absolutely clear vision and brutal honesty if you are to bring about positive change and abundance.

According to this law, self-delusion is the root of all poverty. Let us remember that in the great economic system laid down by God as part of the fundament of the material world, Mind is the currency. Money is merely a physical manifestation of the Mind's power to bring about change. Well, if your mind is locked in on something that denies truth or warps reality, your mental power will buy you exactly what you shop for. In other words, when you are fixed on self-delusion (that which is not real), you manifest that which cannot endure.

You may be thinking, *But I'm no Bernie Madoff. Just as he "used his powers for evil," couldn't I work for good?* In prior teachings, I have

---

2. Bishop John Shelby Spong, *Resurrection: Myth or Reality?* (New York: HarperCollins, 1994), 99.

instructed (and many great New Thought leaders have instructed before me) that with your Divine Mind, when you orient your thoughts to become the thing that you desire and you never waiver, you can achieve virtually anything in this world, even the supposedly impossible. So would it not be possible for an enlightened individual to state his I Am, shape his mind to become the riches he seeks, and bring a 46 percent return on investment into his material experience?

In theory, yes. However, that scenario ignores the fact that no matter how deep and abiding the self-created illusion, *some aspect of the mind always knows the underlying truth.* The Mind is our conduit to God, and God sees through all falsehoods. Even when you are lying to yourself, some part of you knows it. Everyone has experienced this when gambling, trying to lose weight, or assessing a troubled romantic relationship; even when we convince ourselves that everything will be all right, that Divine component of our Mind that cannot be deceived says, "No, this is the truth." Whether we choose to listen or not often determines how our lives progress.

So when you fix your attention on something that appears promising, such as an unheard-of financial return, you may believe that because your Mind is focused on that outcome, it will come to pass. But the Divine Mind knows that your attention is born of fear, desperation, or avarice, and those are the things you will ultimately manifest! *It is impossible to entertain even the deepest self-delusion without part of the Mind knowing the truth.* You are better not to discover your impossible dream at all than to delude yourself into thinking it's real, setting aside all other priorities to bring it into your material reality, and wreaking havoc on your world.

The antidote for this self-destructive pattern is to obey the Law of Clarity and learn to recognize and attend that "still, small voice" that sees through the promises of money, power, and love. Clarity means doing what is alluded to in Matthew in the Bible, removing the plank from your eye so that in all circumstances you can perceive things the way they are, not the way you would wish them to be. Persian poet and mystic Jalal ad-Din Rumi said, "Everyone sees the unseen in proportion to the clarity of his heart, and that depends upon how much he has polished it. Whoever has polished it more sees more—more unseen forms become manifest to him."[3]

SELF-DELUSION ENTANGLES YOU IN LIES

Those who invested with Madoff, who bought homes they could not afford at the urging of unscrupulous mortgage brokers, who spent far beyond their means, discovered one of the basic principles of self-delusion: *it is a communal, collaborative phenomenon.* When you delude yourself about wealth, debt, or an opportunity, you cast your lot in with others doing the same. They are either engaging in and therefore empowering the delusion, or they are manipulating it for their own gain.

Thus, lies breed lies, and the inability to see past one's desires to what is real and in accord with the Divine Will simply spreads the disease. This is obvious when you break down the economic collapse we have experienced, especially as it concerns real estate. If you wanted to take on a mortgage that you could not afford, and you lived on an island, that would only affect your own prosperity. But we are all interconnected, each of us a thread in the great fabric that God is always weaving. Millions of individuals, each thinking he or she was acting alone, took out "toxic" mortgages, and those mortgages then became mortgage-backed securities, which are to blame for much of our national economic crisis. When they defaulted on those mort-

---

3. Jalal al-din Rumi and William C. Chittick, *The Sufi Path of Love* (Albany, NY: SUNY Press, 1983), 162.

gages, the entire house of cards (pun intended) crashed down. Individuals fed the self-delusion and made it grow. That happens in this corporeal life when wishful thinking replaces Divine goals.

Self-delusion entangles you not only in your own lies but in the lies of others. It's not that you cannot use your Mind to bring forth what is improbable. You can! The cosmos is designed for you to tap God's economic stream of Spirit energy to create wealth, security, health, and joy—even if others think you're crazy for wanting a mansion. But the underlying thoughts you hold in your Mind can bless or taint the result, and self-delusion is always based on deception, avarice, and fear. Like crops grown in poisoned soil, what you grow from a desire founded on those thoughts will be unfit.

TO HAVE CLARITY, YOU MUST ALSO HAVE COURAGE

The truth is not always what we would like to have in the short run. We face the constant challenge of having two minds: the mind (lowercase m) that exists in linear time and sees only limitations and lack, and the Mind, our pulsating, living connection to the Almighty that is without time and knows that what we see today is impermanent. Our lives are a constant conflict between our two minds, base and Enlightened.

When we are tempted by that which we know is self-delusion, we allow ourselves to be seduced by the lies because we believe that we do not have the strength or courage to look past what is temporal and fragile and to aspire to what is eternal. The many who bought homes with mortgages they could not afford as soon as the first payment was due did so because they did not trust that they had the strength and courage to go the Divine route, which is more rigorous. They feared that abundance would pass them by and they were not powerful enough to gain what was real by virtue of their own strength.

Taking the Divine path does demand strength and discipline. You must train yourself to set aside what you see and what seems to be wealth for, instead, the wealth of the Mind, and then gradually teach your will to do as God's will does: hold the thing of your desired creation in your Mind's eye and allow the energies of the Universe to accumulate and bring that goal into being. This is not an easy thing do to, but it is truly not beyond the strength of any man or woman. We are all God's children and his proxies in this world, and he has made even the least of us with the potency to manifest that which is good and just. But if someone lacks the courage to take the Enlightened path because she fears failure, then self-delusion and fleeting, empty achievements will be her reward.

Clarity begets honesty begets courage. Once you perceive the truth about an aspiration or opportunity, you cannot be deceived again. Truth cannot become untrue. As former Bishop of Edinburgh Richard Holloway said, "Simplicity, clarity, singleness: These are the attributes that give our lives power and vividness and joy as they are also the marks of great art. They seem to be the purpose of God for His whole creation."[4]

THE SELF-DELUDING ALSO LACK FAITH

Faith is the inner confidence in things unseen. I am not talking about the juvenile faith that some Christians and members of other religions exhibit when they speak of God as a sort of genie in a lamp who grants wishes. That is not God. God is infinitely more complex and subtle, as is the type of faith I speak of. Self-delusion bespeaks

---

4. Helen Coronato, *Eco-Friendly Families* (New York: Penguin, 2008), 56.

of a weak or nonexistent faith in the ecosystem of God, a refusal to believe that the principles of the self-fulfilling Mind can actually be real. It is a refusal to visualize a desire, to orient the Mind on that desire while shifting the essence of one's being to becoming that desire, then to allow the wheels of the Divine to turn and bring that desire into one's experience. Deep down, those who cling to self-delusion delude themselves doubly by believing that God's economy is not real and cannot work.

A husband and wife aspired to buy a home for their family in a place where the fine home they desired was beyond their means. In the beginning, being enlightened people, they made the decision to let their desire come to them. They would adhere to the principles of Mind, focus on their desire, remain courageous, and trust that in time, when they were ready, their dream home would be present in their lives.

But there is no knowing when God's system will act on your behalf. Some desires come about very quickly while others can take years. This is for a very simple yet vital reason: *what you desire will only come when you are morally, emotionally, and spiritually* ready *to receive it.* For example, you might desire a mansion, but if you are not ready for it, you might let it fall into disrepair or allow ownership of such a property to inflate your ego. As I am who I Am, you are ready when you are ready.

As time went by, the couple did not see the dream house coming closer, and slowly lost faith. The two understood that they had to be ready to receive this gift, but they assumed that they already were ready, placing their judgment over God's. In doing this, they lost faith that if they maintained their mental discipline, they would bring about their objective. Instead, they pursued a desperate solution, lied about their income, bought far more home than they could afford, and within a year were in foreclosure.

Their loss of faith caused them to care only about the immediate and ignore the big picture: they had to be the people who were worthy of the gift before the gift would come to them. When we lose faith, we lose it not only in God's system but also in ourselves as custodians of his will.

THE SELF-DELUDED LISTEN NOT TO GOD OR THEMSELVES, BUT TO OTHERS

Self-delusion is a collaborative act. We rarely lie to ourselves about things within our own grasp; we require others to present us with options that are just outside the realm of possibility. We give their words credence and slowly, over time, we lose the ability to hear what New Thought scholars have called the "Divine voice of wisdom" ringing in our own ears. We become deaf to the voice of God speaking through our instincts, that inner voice that cannot be fooled and knows when we are hitching our wagon to something fragile and ephemeral. When enough others pursue what appears simple and rewarding, we begin to question whether our inner wisdom—our common sense—is worth listening to. We stop paying attention to God's system and instead use that attention to buy what cannot possibly last.

The story of the economic collapse that has afflicted our world culture is a story of people allowing themselves to grow deaf to Divine wisdom by embracing self-delusion. Clarity is a gift: the power to see things not only as they truly are but as they truly can be. But that potential comes with rigor and discipline, as I have said. There is no easy, slothful path to the things you want for your life and the lives of the people you love. There is only growth and sacrifice and the rejection of the easy and temporary in favor of the deep-rooted and fulfilling.

Attention is currency, because whatever you focus your Mind on will come to pass in your experience. That is why we use the phrase "pay attention." When your attention shifts from your inner voice to the blandishments of those who want you to walk the easy path away from Spirit, you pay for the destination that path ends at. In the short term, yes, that path can appear to deliver treasures: a new house, a new car, or a flourishing investment portfolio. But what will happen in the long term? A spirit deaf to eternal wisdom finds only dust and might-have-beens: lost cars, lost homes, lost savings, lost jobs, lost futures, and lost hope.

The legacy of the world's financial meltdowns is one of shattered illusions and fallen gurus. The Bible tells us not to put our faith in the princes of this world, and the financial gods of Wall Street had become, in effect, princes of prosperity. Yet they proved fallible because anything based on the corporeal human brain is fallible; we are flesh and we fail and err and die. Only the Mind that is woven into God's reality is eternal and infallible. When we listen to that voice with clarity and courage, we cannot be steered down a destructive path. We might hear what we do not want to hear, such as, "No, you cannot have that now because you are not ready." But that is an opportunity to keep faith, find strength, and stay the course. Eventually each of us becomes ready for what we desire ... if we listen to Divine wisdom and discipline our Minds.

DESIRES BORN OF CLARITY BRING GROWTH

Are the rich happier than the rest of us? That is an eternal question, and I think most people who are not rich would say, "Yes, of course they are!" After all, the rich don't have to worry about paying the mortgage, having the car repossessed, or filing for unemployment benefits. But when you look closer at the lives of the wealthy, you see a disparity that makes the principles of the Law of Clarity come into sharp focus.

On one hand, you see people like my great friend Russell Simmons. This is a man who came from nothing and yet with his will and his faith has created not just wealth, not just a business and entertainment empire, but prosperity for himself and others. But (and this is key) he has built a *life* that is not about wealth and prosperity. It is about values, generosity, joy, and creation. Those are the hallmarks of someone who took the path of clarity, listened to his inner voice, did not engage in self-delusion, and crafted a reality that is rich in the deeper ways of Spirit. If you took everything away from Russell tomorrow, he would still consider himself wealthy, because of what he has given back, the opportunity he has made for others, and the ways in which he has grown in Mind, vision, and faith.

Contrast this with those who took the easy way to riches, who deluded themselves that investing in a "bubble" or playing illegal games with the stock market would yield lasting prosperity. The folly of this approach shows itself in several ways. First of all, when riches are gained in such a manner, they are purely superficial; the person gaining them has not grown or become wiser in the process, which leaves him or her vulnerable to circumstances. Second, the wealth does not create joy but more often anxiety, envy, and stress because the things of Spirit—purpose, passion, love—have been sacrificed at the altar of bringing home a fat paycheck. Finally, when adversity strikes and the edifice comes crashing down (as has happened to many formerly rich Americans), the person either panics or denies what is happening. The result is utter personal and financial ruin.

The process of following the road of mental discipline and Spirit, using God's economic system, conditions the person who follows it to grow immensely by the time he or she reaches fulfillment of a desire. Remember, riches are different for each of us; the person who desires a simple home, freedom from debt and a healthy and loving family is no less wise than the person who wants to be a millionaire. Wealth, in the context of the Laws of Prosperity, is defined as *the state in which one spends each day in a place of continual, profound gratitude.*

Does that sound anything like a description of wealth you have heard before? I expect not, because so many people are obsessed with the self-delusion that making more money will put them in that sublime state of lasting gratitude. It can, but it often does not. You must discover what prosperity means for you and then honor the path to that prosperity, even though it may not be easy.

There are many ways to be wealthy. The millionaire can be happy if he has been true to the path and grown wiser and more compassionate as his bank account has grown. So the starving artist can be wealthy if she spends her time doing what she loves, and the blue-collar worker can be wealthy if he has a secure job, a roof over his head, and a loving family. Shedding self-delusion and adhering to clarity always brings outcomes of growth, joy, and wisdom.

How can you leverage the Law of Clarity in your own journey to become more united with your Divine Mind and to bring prosperity to your life? Let me begin by stating some assumptions that apply to every chapter and every Law in this book:

- I believe you are economically or financially dissatisfied in some way.
- I believe you wish to change your current situation by assertive action and new thinking.
- I believe you are familiar with the Divine economy and the Laws of Mind.

I recommend reading my earlier bestseller, *The Laws of Thinking*, before you progress with this book. But if you have a passing acquaintance with the manner in which Mind manifests via your *I Am* identity, then you can put the Law of Clarity to work to help bring prosperity into your orbit.

What We Have Learned

- Self-delusion is merely an escape, a means of avoiding reality because you doubt your ability to survive and thrive.

- The Mind always sees through delusion and manifests the emotions behind the delusion.

- Courage, faith, the ability to listen to your Divine Voice of Wisdom, and constant attention to your true desires are needed to resist self-delusion and reap the rewards.

- Clarity breeds outcomes that bring joy, growth, and satisfaction.

2

THE LAW OF
COMPENSATION

■ ■ ■ ■ ■

CORE PRINCIPLES

- The life of the Spirit is one of eternal balance between good and evil, plenty and lack.

- When one thing departs your life, another always enters.

- You must use your Mind to determine the nature of the new thing entering your life.

It is the old statement that water will reach its own level by its own weight, and without effort. So a treatment will only level itself in the objective world at the level of the subjective thought and realization. This does not mean that [a person] will always have to receive the same compensation . . . With an enlarged consciousness he would receive more.

—Ernest Holmes and Maude Allison Latham, *The Science of Mind*

We are accustomed to framing the concept of compensation as payment: money given for services or products rendered. But that is a simplistic version of a grander idea that misses the entire point of compensation and its relation to God's economy. Indeed, compensation is a core principle of managing your life in this physical world and in the world of Spirit!

The more relevant, truer meaning of the word *compensation* is "balance." It's as simple as Newtonian physics: for every action, there is an equal and opposite reaction. When you do a deed of kindness for another person without expecting a reward, you find rewards coming your way. The fundamental state of the cosmos is balance, which is why all things physical come into being and eventually die. The universe is an engine of creation, but for each thing created, something must be annihilated. Everything goes toward maintaining the balance.

When we peer beneath the surface with this kind of understanding, each human enterprise is about compensating for one thing or another in order to keep the balance. Medicine appears to be about diagnosis and treatment, but in its purest form, it is about restoring the body's natural balance to foster well-being. This essential balancing act may be most visible in law. Society's laws exist to maintain the equilibrium between chaos and order, sin and justice.

A typical example: A man commits a crime. He is apprehended by law enforcement, charged, and put on trial. Eventually, if he is guilty of the crime, he is convicted and a sentence is handed down. Punishment is compensation to the victim, the victim's family, and society as a whole for the chaos—the entropy—introduced into the world by the criminal. With the application of punishment, whether it be a prison sentence or a financial cost, order and balance are restored. The cosmos cannot maintain itself any other way.

LIVING WITH COMPENSATION

Living with compensation is a principle that is as vital to the operating clockwork of the universe as gravity is on earth. It also affects the ups and downs of your life and of your financial future.

THE LAW OF COMPENSATION

When someone or something leaves your experience,
someone or something new always enters. Your state
of Mind will determine its nature and whether
it is beneficial or detrimental.

This principle is perhaps on display most clearly (and most appropriately during these economic times) in the loss of employment. This plague, which is affecting millions of people, comes with its symptoms: the ailing company finances, the warnings of downsizing, the drop in the stomach that comes with a layoff notice, the panic over not being able to make the mortgage payment. But if you can step back from the experience, job loss is simply something leaving your life. Something new will be entering to compensate. What will it be?

The rules of God's economy dictate that your Mind determines what enters your life when something departs. If your attention is focused on hopelessness, despair, and desperation, then that is what you attract. The new presence in your experience might then be foreclosure, disease, the loss of your spouse's job, or some other financial catastrophe. On the other hand, if you can discipline your Mind and surpass the circumstances of the moment to orient your mental force on hope, opportunity, and creativity, then those qualities will infuse the newness that comes into your world. This is how losing a job can be a gateway to starting a prosperous new business, discovering a cherished passion, or finding a new way to live by helping others.

The great Catherine Ponder said, "If you want greater prosperity in your life, start forming a vacuum to receive it."[1] Nature abhors a vacuum, so it rushes to fill each one. In this case, that vacuum is loss, which is why we should pay attention to the powerful Buddhist concept of nonattachment. Buddhists believe that all suffering in the world is caused by our attachment to things, including our selves and our lives. We try to prevent loss in our lives as a kind of reflex, without considering that such loss may be the will of God, a part of our destiny.

When you view attachment as a barrier to the new good or prosperity that may be waiting to enter your life, you will become more willing to accept losses as they come and for what they are: the clearing of dead brush so that new blessings may grow. As long as

---

1. Catherine Ponder, *The Dynamic Laws of Prosperity* (Camarillo, CA: DeVorss, 1985), 41.

your experience is overgrown by that which steals your attention and distracts you from the purpose of honing your Mind to serve the mission of God, you block the new good from growing into your life. As long as you orient yourself on that which is dark—death, loss, pain, want—you allow only the same kinds of seeds to flourish in your garden.

CHOOSING THE OUTCOME

ESPY-winning triathlete Jason Lester, one of the world's greatest extreme-distance racers and the first challenged athlete to finish an Ultraman race (a double triathlon), does not have the use of his right arm. The arm was paralyzed when he was hit by a car at twelve years old. If he had chosen to focus on the loss of an arm—which would have been understandable at an age when his thoughts were probably all about sports—what would he have manifested in his future? Pity, hopelessness, disability, and anger. Losing the use of his arm was a wrenching, painful departure from his experience, but what came into his experience could have been even worse.

Instead, Lester chose to focus on running and competing—on what he could do, not what he could not do. He became an all-star football and baseball player and later fulfilled God's plan for him by becoming a world-class distance athlete and an inspiration to millions of people with and without physical challenges. He's even written a book, *Running on Faith*. His positive, hopeful state of mind, which he carried with him even during dark times of pain and regret, eventually manifested great good, hope, and accomplishment. That is what is possible when you understand how the Law of Compensation works.

Compensation allows you to choose the outcome of events in your life and to ordain them for the greater good of God. Framing the losses of your experience not as "something was taken from me" but as "something was cleared from my life so that something better may enter" directs the creative energies of Spirit to coalesce into something wondrous and positive that more than compensates you for that which you lost. For example:

- You are laid off from your job. After the initial shock, you decide to orient your Mind not on the loss but on the potential to pursue a living in line with your deepest passions. In a matter of weeks, the perfect job comes seemingly from nowhere.
- Your marriage ends badly. Instead of blaming and seeking out desperate solace by jumping into a rebound relationship, you look to improve yourself and focus on becoming the finest person you can be. In a short time, someone new enters your life who is suited for the stronger, wiser individual you have become.
- A loved one passes from this physical life. You grieve the loss temporarily, but you also take up the work that the person did to help poor students get a better education. This positive approach to death breeds a life-affirming response from the Universe: the organization your loved one once aided now asks you to become formally involved, lending a new sense of purpose and fulfillment to your life as you help others.

In each of these scenarios, things could have turned out very differently. The job loss could have spiraled into bankruptcy and depression. The broken relationship could have led to violence or addiction. The loss of a loved one could have sparked a bottomless pit of grief. In all cases, we have the power to choose the outcome, choose what comes next.

This is not anything so simplistic as "making lemonade out of lemons." Leveraging the Law of Compensation means more than putting on a brave face after a disaster and fighting through depression or fear. It means transforming your mind to hold the unshakable knowledge—the surety—that compensation is coming to balance the scales and what does come will be wondrous and surprising in ways that you cannot imagine. It is knowing and believing without exception that the cosmos is bound by its maker to compensate for anything that leaves your life, and that the compensation is determined by the state of your enlightenment—and of your spirit. The brighter you shine, the brighter your future.

Physicist Nikola Tesla said, "My belief is firm in a law of compensation. The true rewards are ever in proportion to the labor and sacrifices made."[2] Tesla was one of the prime decoders of the nature of the universe, and he understood the meaning of compensation. One of the truths he and others like him came to realize was this: *that which enters your life does not have to equal that which has departed.*

Do you understand how crucial this is? There is no guarantee of equivalence. In other words, when you lose a job, there is nothing in the Law that says a job of equal quality or pay must come into your experience. It could be a lesser job or a much greater opportunity. With your Mind, you have the ability to determine whether your compensation will advance you to a new level, have you treading water, or actually set you back. A seemingly lesser job and greater one can both do any of these things.

This is what Tesla meant by "labor and sacrifices made." We must labor with our Minds to discipline our thoughts and concentrate our attention on shaping that which is inbound to our lives.

---

2. Nikola Tesla, *My Inventions: The Autobiography of Nikola Tesla* (New York: Cosimo, 2007), 69.

We must also sacrifice the typical, unenlightened responses to loss: grief, blame, anger, despair, and escape. These feelings are luxuries that we cannot afford, because they will taint the incoming balance. In directing your own prosperity and dealing with your own losses, ask yourself: *How am I using my Mind to transform the energy of departure into the hope of new arrival? What kind of compensation am I commanding?*

MASTERS OF COMPENSATION OFTEN BECOME ENTREPRENEURS

Entrepreneurship is not about starting a small business. It is about creating something out of nothing to fill a need. The most powerful engine of entrepreneurship is not inspiration or business skill but failure—the act of losing one's idea, money, or opportunity. Ask the most successful entrepreneurs you know; they all will tell you that abject failures preceded their greatest triumphs.

You know the fast-food chain KFC, right? Well, it was not always the booming enterprise it is today. When he was sixty-five, Harland Sanders's restaurant/gas station folded because the new interstate highway system bypassed it. He had nothing but a Social Security check, an old car, and a chicken recipe. He could have surrendered to poverty and resentment, but instead he and his wife went on the road, calling on restaurant owners to try to convince them to buy his recipe in exchange for a royalty on chicken sold. They slept in the car to save money. Of his first 1,008 sales calls, do you know how many said yes? Zero. That's right. Who among us would have the fortitude to persevere in the face of that much crippling rejection?

Colonel Sanders did. He knew that if he was to create something new from the loss of his business, he had to use his Mind to bind the good that could come. The 1,009th prospect agreed to a deal, and as the word got out about the chicken, more deals followed. Over the next two decades, Harlan built his recipe into a multimillion-dollar business.

This is a vital anecdote because the spirit of entrepreneurship is the spirit of self-creation and self-reinvention. If you lose something from your life, especially your means of financial support, and your Mind is directed toward reaching for a life preserver out of desperation, what do you end up doing? You attract something desperate into your existence and end up with the same kind of disposable, dead-end job you had before. You do not advance toward Enlightenment and a greater ability to fulfill your part of God's Purpose. However, if you have an entrepreneurial mind and can see the opportunity in failure and loss, you manifest something that opens new doors and creates new opportunities for you not only to earn a living but to grow your understanding of God's Laws and your place within them.

New Thought pioneer Orison Swett Marden wrote, "Many a man has finally succeeded only because he has failed after repeated efforts. If he had never met defeat he would never have known any great victory."[3]

THE LAW OF COMPENSATION WILL NEVER BRING YOU NOTHING

There is a saying in the business world: "Advertising never doesn't work." That means that when you put an advertising message out into the world, it always has an effect. It just might not be the effect you imagined or intended. The Law of Compensation is the same

---

3. http://quotationbook.com (accessed August 12, 2009).

way. It always brings something into your experience to replace something that has left your experience. It is always functioning, always waiting. It is impossible for it not to fill that void with some kind of freshly manifested potential, relationship, or reality.

The American Trappist monk Thomas Merton said, "Happiness is not a matter of intensity but of balance, order, rhythm, and harmony."[4] The Law of Compensation is continuously ticking away to maintain that balance and harmony despite the chaotic nature of human life on this physical plane. That means that when something exits your life, you do not get to choose whether or not something else will come to fill that void. Compensation ensures it in accordance with the structure of the cosmos that God laid down at the creation. You cannot get a pass from this; as soon as you lose a relationship or even a possession, the etheric gears and machinery begin pulsing and turning in order to bring someone or something else into your awareness. Whether you want it to or not, this will happen.

This means that while you have a personal responsibility to govern the power of your Divine Mind to manifest your thoughts as reality at all times, this responsibility becomes especially keen when there is a void in your life. That void is temporary. The great engine of universal creation is hard at work turning out some new experience to keep your life balanced, so it is at this time more than any other that you must discipline, order, and orient your thoughts on creating abundance, health, and prosperity. It is not possible for the cosmos not to bring something new into your world. The Law of Compensation works its wonders whether we want it to or not.

As an example appropriate to these difficult times, let us postulate that you lose your home to foreclosure, a terrible and humiliating

---

4. Thomas Merton, *No Man Is an Island* (Boston: Shambahala Publications, 2005), 134.

ordeal to endure. But in the wake of that loss, you don't respond by wrenching your mind into a hopeful and productive state. Instead, you choose to hibernate. You retreat from the reality of what has happened in search of a "break" from the harshness of your situation. In doing so, you are like a driver taking his hands off the wheel of a car going seventy miles per hour. You are abdicating any control over what happens.

Even inviting negative consequences into your experience is better than inviting unknown chaos by refusing to think about the loss and what comes next. The void will be filled. If you don't fill it with the product of your mental activity, the new influence in your life will come about from the thoughts and intentions of the people around you. Ask yourself, would you rather trust your God-created Mind to shape your future or the random—perhaps poisonous— thoughts of those around you? Even a friend's well-meaning, "Poor you!" is toxic in this example.

COMPENSATION SOMETIMES BRINGS YOU SOMETHING SIMILAR, SOMETHING OPPOSITE, OR SOMETHING TOTALLY DIFFERENT

We have all known of this person before: the jilted woman whose man leaves her for another. The woman discovers that her companion was untrue or unworthy once their relationship ends. She struggles with loneliness and the fear of growing old alone, and she vows that she will never again fall for the same sort of man. Yet within a few months, she is with a new man who is a virtual carbon copy of the man she dumped. Why? Because she did not change her thoughts about the type of person who was right for her. Her mind remained fixed on finding a new man who was just like the old one. Therefore, she attracted the same sort of man to fill that void. If your mind remains firmly focused on manifesting the identical thing that recently exited your experience, you can be sure you will find it coming into your life. On the other hand, if you let your mental energies "float" without purpose or intent, then you may attract something rather different from what you knew. In other words, this is not a cosmic photocopy service; it's not "lose a job, gain a job" unless you have a powerful and unrelenting desire to make it so. It is possible to see a relationship depart from your life and then to see economic opportunity enter. The key is this: *what enters your experience to fill a vacuum tends to be whatever best serves your role in God's purpose at the time.* Lose a job, gain a family heirloom; lose some aspect of your health to disease, gain a new purpose in helping others with the same disease—compensation is often not direct, not one thing for an identical thing. Very frequently, what enters your awareness to maintain the balance is something in another area of life. So a job might compensate you for a lost relationship, or a new spiritual awareness might come to you as compensation for lost employment.

What will never change, however, is the nature of the compensatory force that enters your life. Its fundamental nature will match the tuning and frame of your Divine Mind in perfect harmony, for better or worse. What do I mean by that? If, after you suffer a layoff from your job, you focus your attention on poverty and depression, even if what comes into your life to compensate you for that lost job is a new relationship, that relationship will be based on poverty and depression. If you are diagnosed with cancer and have to lose part of your body in an effort to cure it, something else will arrive in your experience as compensation. If your mental force is positive, purposeful and life-affirming, whatever form that new thing takes will also be positive, purposeful, and life-affirming. The form can be different; the nature is always determined by the status of your Mind.

THOSE WHO DO ILL ARE NOT COMPENSATED WITH WEALTH

In April of 2009, David Kellerman, the acting chief financial officer of the huge government-backed mortgage lender Freddie Mac, committed suicide. He was burdened by the collapse of the company under mountains of toxic debt and apparently could not take the knowledge that he had been partially responsible for the nation's economic meltdown. This was a man who, by all accounts, was wealthy and powerful and enjoyed a high level of status among his peers on Wall Street. Yet he felt pain extreme enough to surrender God's greatest gift, life. Why?

This pattern has revealed itself over and over again among the financial elite since the economy began to slide into deep, painful recession. We have read about top bankers, stockbrokers, and money managers—the "smartest guys in the room" who were in part responsible for the greed and irresponsible risk that brought down America's financial house of cards—taking their own lives, sliding into depression, developing substance addictions, and more. For those with the most, the loss of everything always proves more agonizing than it is for those who have little to lose.

The point of this is not to engage in what the Germans call *schadenfreude*, delight in someone else's deserved misfortune. It is to illustrate that while we may think millionaire Wall Street titans have been rewarded for misdeeds that took away the jobs and homes of millions of hardworking people, in most cases this is illusion. Remember, the underlying orientation of the Mind is what determines what manifests in the lives of everyone, including the superrich. It has been well-documented that many of those who lived high and mighty during the economic bubble actually already had terrible marital discord, addictions, deep personal debt, horrible moral conflicts, health troubles, and so on. A mentality focused on avarice and on creating wealth for ourselves by taking from others might produce short-term materialistic gains, but it also invites compensation that reflects those values.

So a wealthy financial guru who has made his fortune through illegal means might see his ethical center depart his life, and the compensation might be yet someone else's illegal activity robbing him of his money. Someone obsessed with working and making money might spend so much time at the office that his relationships with his children deteriorate, and the compensation for that neglect is family chaos. There is a price for all things, and with wealth the price is often cripplingly high. Do not envy the wealthy elite without knowing what is happening behind their closed doors and in their Spirits. Ask yourself who is richer: the wise working-class man who understands the power of his Divine Mind and uses it to maintain a happy family, a healthy body, and an honest, decent job, or a rich man with a mansion and a Bentley, whose children despise him, who has high blood pressure and heart disease due to stress, and who wakes up every day hating his place in the world?

COMPENSATION MEANS HELPING OTHERS AVOID NEGATIVE THINKING AFTER A LOSS

As these tumultuous economic times persist and spread their damage throughout our civilization, we have the misfortune to watch not only our own futures made vulnerable but those of the people around us. And as so often proves true, the unenlightened are the victims not only of outside influence but of their own toxic Minds, which attracts into their orbits the lack and misfortune upon which their thoughts dwell. It is painful to watch someone fall prey to her own lack of understanding that she is her own devil and not the victim of some outside imp born in biblical myth. However, there is much we can do.

It remains true that each person is the captain of his or her own soul, and so one can ultimately only save oneself. But each of us has a duty not only to see to our own enlightenment within the economic system of God but also to shepherd others the way a financial custodian manages the affairs of his or her clients. When someone in your circle or community or church is suffering from a loss, it is incumbent upon you to remind that person to fix his or her Mind on possibility and creation and to remind the person that the Law of Compensation is already at work, knitting the fabric of reality into a new manifestation.

This is how we can prevent those we love and cherish from falling into the same traps again and again. Patterns of thinking, after all, produce patterns of manifestation; thus do individuals who chronically lose their jobs seem to bounce from situation to situation, constantly sabotaging their own fortunes. In fact, though this has not yet been convincingly demonstrated, I believe that part of the Law of Compensation may be that the more you repeat the same loss-to-compensation cycle, the more you reinforce the nature of your compensation. So the more often you respond to something exiting your life with a mental position of hope, empowerment, and creativity, the easier it may become for the cosmos to manifest good and abundance in your experience. Obviously, the reverse may also be true.

The self-reinforcing nature of compensation means that we owe it to our fellow travelers through this physical plane to help them train their minds on pulling that which enhances and grows their being in the wake of loss. This can be as simple as the reminder that loss is often a gateway to greater good and greater fortunes.

Putting the Law of Compensation to Work

There are two ways to leverage the Law of Compensation. First, you can train your Mind to release those reflexive feelings of grief and anger over a temporal loss. The feelings are manifestations of the physical body's attachment to the things of the flesh. Change is so wrenching because we do not want to give up our comforts and the familiar. However, if we remember that all things come to us via the grace of God's system, we will understand those things are all temporary and designed to serve a greater good: our development into superior vessels for a part of God's Divine Design. Everything comes into and leaves our lives at an ordained time and for an ordained reason, though the webs may be so complex that we cannot perceive that reason.

The way to develop this understanding is primarily through prayer or meditation. Develop your own discipline that allows you to quiet your conscious mind and tap into that Spirit level of consciousness that reveals the flow of energy that is always waiting to manifest in your experience. Train your mind to focus on this energy and the eternal nature of humanity's Spirit. This will help you put the petty losses and gains of physical life into perspective and remember even in dark times that when God closes a door, he inevitably opens a window.

The other means to develop a powerful adeptness with compensation is simply to review the times in your life when you have suffered losses and examine your mind-set following that loss and what results came from that mind-set. For example, a writer I have worked with many times over the years told me that he felt fated to jump from bad relationship to bad relationship until one day, after another bad breakup, he had an epiphany: he was not taking responsibility for his own joy in his relationships. Rather than wait for some other force to make him happy, he decided then and there to transform his Mind before he entered another relationship. He did so, and shortly afterward he met the woman who became his wife—who lived on his street, fewer than two hundred feet from his home, but whom he had never seen before. She had been in front of his eyes for three years but he could not perceive her until he was ready—until the cosmos brought him the awareness to perceive a wonderful woman with his new eyes.

WHAT WE HAVE LEARNED

- Compensation is always at work as soon as you experience a loss; it is vital to maintain cosmic balance.

- Your compensation will reflect how you react to loss.

- Losses are temporary and can be gateways to great growth and abundance if you let go of attachment.

- You have the power to choose the outcome.

- Repeated compensation establishes patterns that reinforce the nature of what you will experience.

3

THE LAW OF DEBT

■ ■ ■ ■ ■

CORE PRINCIPLES

- Life is an act of running up debt.

- You cannot escape your obligations to the debt you incur in life.

- Your debts must be paid voluntarily or they will be paid against your will.

The whole of what we know is a system of compensations. Each suffering is rewarded; each sacrifice is made up; every debt is paid.

—Ralph Waldo Emerson

Debtor's prison. Indentured servitude to pay off a debt in default. Certainly, the toxic debt of subprime mortgage loans that was partially to blame for our economic crisis. Debt is a hot issue and an ancient one; as far back as the first century BC, Roman author Publilius Syrus said, "Debt is the slavery of the free."[1] For millennia, human beings have been interested in possessing as much as we possibly can in the earthly economy. Even George Washington became obsessed with acquiring land. Dutch speculators drove the price of a single tulip bulb to ridiculous heights that would not be seen again until our modern real estate bubble. Like a rabbit staring down a cobra, we stare down debt, spending ourselves to the outermost limit of our means and then, if we are fortunate, we back down in time and can pay our bills, only to run up debt again as soon as we feel solvent.

It is a dangerous game, made more so because in focusing on earthly debt, we ignore the cosmic debt that we must pay in life. That debt consists of obligations that we owe to the Universe in return for the things we are granted. To whom much is granted,

---

1. http://thinkexist.com (accessed August 21, 2009).

much is expected. We are no exception. The blessings of God yielded to us through the clockwork system of the cosmos are not free; we must pay for them in ways that have nothing to do with money. Yet the mechanics behind earthly debt and etheric debt have their similarities, and it is these that inform this chapter.

The concept of debt is perhaps best expressed by the story of Abraham, who was willing to sacrifice his beloved son Isaac to God because he felt the obligation of obedience. Abraham was well aware that he owed literally everything, his very being, to God and therefore bore a cosmic debt that had to be repaid. He knew that if he did not repay it on God's terms as an act of his own free will, the debt would come to term in a way over which he had no control, and that the consequences might be dire indeed. So he took his only son to the mountain, bound him, and prepared to sacrifice him as a burned offering. In the face of what had to have been crippling emotional agony, Abraham's knowledge that he must repay his debt was all-powerful—and his intent to fulfill that obligation was the key.

As we know, the angel of the Lord stopped Abraham from slaying his son, and God rewarded him for his faith and trust:

> *The angel of the Lord called to Abraham from heaven a second time and said, "I swear by myself, declares the Lord, that because you have done this and have not withheld your son, your only son, I will surely bless you and make your descendants as numerous as the stars in the sky and as the sand on the seashore. Your descendants will take possession of the cities of their enemies, and through your offspring all nations on earth will be blessed, because you have obeyed me." (Genesis 22:15-18)*

It is the pure intent to repay our cosmic debt to God—more to the point, to God's ticking, always-operating system—that wins us freedom and riches. As in life, we cannot avoid debt, but we can act with honor and awareness that the debt we take on must be balanced in the reward it offers and must be repaid in kind.

A Matter of Humility

The Law of Debt in relation to the prosperity that we manifest with the Divine Mind has nothing whatsoever to do with credit cards, loans, or banks.

The Law of Debt

The nature of the cosmos and God's economy means that you will be indebted to someone or something at all times, and that debt will be repaid without exception.

In a very real way, this Law is a counterpart to the Law of Compensation. But with debt, we are the ones providing the compensation, not the cosmos. Remember, all things must balance or else everything becomes chaos. Cosmos is the opposite of chaos—the implicit order of all things under the Laws of God represented by the Laws of Nature. The balance is always maintained, with our cooperation or despite us. Therefore, just as we receive compensation when something departs our lives, we must also compensate the Universe for that which we receive. Much is expected of us.

The central principle that underlies this law is humility. In order to understand the importance of repaying a debt, you must be humble enough to acknowledge that you are beholden to the provider of whatever you have received. You must avoid the arrogance that says, "I am the source of all the good that has come into my life." This loss of perspective leads to a refusal to acknowledge that a debt must always be met. This is precisely what has occurred in so many segments of the mortal economy as everyone from bankers to homeowners assumed that they, rather than God's system in its endless cycles, were the cause of the wealth that manifested in their experiences.

In refusing to be humble and fulfill their obligations to maintain the balance, many people were brought low by their hubris, descending into poverty, loss, and pain. You see, the accounts of the Divine system are always settled; as with other Laws, the action is unstoppable and continuous. You cannot avoid repayment. However, where human free will comes into play is this: *we possess the freedom to choose the manner of repayment.*

If we maintain humility and perspective and choose to settle our obligations in a way that is honest and done with an open heart, then we maintain control. Yet, if we slough off our obligations, then the same thing that happens in the physical world of finance can occur: what we have is forcibly ripped from us. This is the spiritual meaning of the word *repossession. To possess* in spiritual terms is "to inhabit," as in the way that we are physical shells inhabited by Spirit. In the transactions of the Divine Mind, when we cannot or will not meet our obligations, we may be re-possessed, meaning that a different aspect of Spirit takes up residence in us and denies us the ability to manifest the prosperity or well-being that we once had.

This is why people who over-leveraged themselves in the monetary world could and did fall so quickly to ruin: they literally became different people who lost the "magic touch" of creating wealth. When they refused to meet their obligations, that gift was stripped away.

Spiritual Meets Financial

Earth gets its price for what Earth gives us,
The beggar is taxed for a corner to die in,
The priest hath his fee who comes and shrives us,
We bargain for the graves we lie in;
At the devil's booth are all things sold,
Each ounce of dross costs its ounce of gold;
For a cap and bells our lives we pay.
Bubbles we buy with a whole soul's tasking,
'Tis heaven alone that is given away,
'Tis only God may be had for the asking,
No price is set on the lavish summer;
June may be had by the poorest comer.

— James Russell Lowell, "The Vision of Sir Launfal"

There is a price for all things; nothing is free, and what you get is worth what you pay for it. This is why those riches that are only gained through the efforts of the physical are fleeting, while wealth created through the Divine Mind is lasting. Just as in the material world, what you get is probably worth what you paid for it. In fact, there are many similarities between the spiritual type of debt and the world of finance. I will explore two of the most important.

In the financial world, debt is often taken on—particularly as a home mortgage—with the signing of a trust deed. Think about the meaning of those words: *trust deed*. An action that implies trustworthiness and must be supported by continued trustworthy action. In the spiritual realm, abundance is granted to you by the cosmos with the assumption that you will perform deeds that can be trusted to repay the universal order for that which you receive. Basically, the Universe is trusting you to say, "Thank you!" When you don't, you are in default, and problems arise.

The other critical term of similarity is *interest rate*. In finance, the interest rate is the amount of money a lender makes as your cost of borrowing still more money—a direct violation of the ancient Hebrew prohibition against usury. In the spiritual realm, interest rate also reflects a cost—the cost you must pay for the blessings of your life by showing interest in and paying attention to your Divine Mind's development.

You see, God's economic system does not grant you wealth, health, and joy for their own sake; God is interested in seeing you grow in Spirit as a perfect vessel of his will. You must take this same interest or you are violating the Spirit in which the gifts of your life have been given. Your "rate of interest" usually determines whether you will appreciate the gifts of God in such a way that you will repay them appropriately.

These two powerful examples illustrate the perfect parallels between earthly debt and obligation and those that filter down to us from above. In both, we must prove ourselves worthy of trust and pay interest, or there is an additional charge.

OUR OBLIGATIONS AND PAYMENT

Guru Sri Sathya Sai Baba said, "Concern for one's own welfare and prosperity should not blind one to one's social obligations or spiritual destiny ... A society in which the individuals are concerned only about material welfare will not be able to achieve harmony and peace."[2] Our obligations to God are not about material blessings, but spiritual ones. But what are some of our blessings and how must they be repaid?

One example of a person solving this vital equation is Millard Fuller, founder of Habitat for Humanity. A graduate of Auburn

---

2. http://saibaba.ws (accessed August 3, 2009).

University and the University of Alabama Law School, Fuller applied his business expertise and entrepreneurial drive vigorously, becoming a millionaire at age twenty-nine. But his health, ethical sense, and marriage suffered, and he had the perspective to reassess his life and devote himself to others—to pay back what he had received in service. "I see life as both a gift and a responsibility. My responsibility is to use what God has given me to help his people in need,"[3] he said. In the next chapter, we'll discuss why you need to care about more than yourself. These are some of our primary obligations and repayments:

Manifestation—We inherit the natural power to manifest wealth, opportunity, relationships, health, and much more from the ether. Our obligation for the incredible gift of manifestation is to manifest that which enhances the world around us and help others reach their own God-given destiny. For example, manifesting wealth only centered on yourself would be defaulting on this promise, while manifesting wealth that benefits the community would be a trust deed.

Purpose—We are granted a place in God's purpose, which in turn gives our lives on the physical plane form and direction. We are each God's proxies on this earth, charged with a small piece of His design. As such, our part is to devote our time to the fulfillment of that purpose, known only to each of us by means of prayer or meditation. This, then, is the price of purpose: prayer.

Life—The greatest gift of all is ours, the opportunity to exist as independent beings of free will and the chance to grow and come

---

3. http://www.habitat.org (accessed August 1, 2009).

into our power. It is truly extraordinary! In return for the gift of life, our part is to do two things for God:

1. We must grow into our Divine nature throughout life, progressing as best we can toward a higher spiritual evolution. We will fail at times but, as with Abraham, it is the intent that matters.

2. We must die and pass from this physical plane to take what we have learned and reunite with the cosmic Consciousness that is God. Death is the high cost of living. It comes as a part of the natural cycle when we have finally reached the point where we can no longer grow in this material world.

The issues related to spiritual debt have a close and relevant relationship to the financial travails of our current culture. The same dynamic that results in the accumulation of spiritual debt produces financial debt: arrogance, lack of perspective, refusal to accept responsibility. That debt occurs not only because of reckless spending decisions but because of a lack of understanding of purpose. When we labor under the misconception that our purpose is defined by what we spend and own rather than how well we serve God's purpose, we are destined for debt.

WHEN WE CAN DEFAULT ON OUR OBLIGATIONS TO GOD

The question of defaulting on our obligations is a complex one. On one hand, we can indeed default on God's loan of life and manifestation, when we refuse to render the proper spiritual compensation: growth, contributing to the community, risk taking, fostering the spiritual development of others. We then go into default and risk negative outcomes. But in another way, we cannot default, because unlike earthly fiscal debt, which in some cases is never collected, the cosmos will always take compensation from us in some form. It just may not be in the form that we desire.

Again, the Law of Debt is a counterpart to the Law of Compensation and features the same around-the-clock mechanism humming away beneath the visible operation of Nature. Just as compensation is automatic when something leaves our experience, debt produces a debit from our lives to repay the cost of what we have gained. The key comes in this question: do we consciously repay the debt and control the price the Universe exacts from us, or do we ignore the debt and allow the Universe to debit our life account in a way that we cannot predict?

What happens when we go into default? We lose all control over what will be taken from us in compensation for what we have received. This is the source of much of the misfortune that befalls individuals who become blinded by greed and think that financial acquisition is the only purpose in life. As New Thought author Eric Butterworth wrote, "Prosperity is a way of living and thinking, and not just money or things. Poverty is a way of living and thinking, and not just a lack of money or things."[4] When we forget this and the cosmic debt comes due, the cosmos will debit us whatever balances our accounts.

Thus, riches can vanish in a storm of corruption. Housing prices can collapse. Stock markets can tumble. Businesses can fail. Marriages can crumble, taking the household down through the expensive pain of divorce. When you refuse to pay your debts in the physical world, you go into collections and systems beyond your control can garnish your wages, damage your credit, and wreck your

---

4. Eric Butterworth, *Spiritual Economics: The Principles and Process of True Prosperity* (Unity Village, MO: Unity Books, 2001), 10.

life. The same thing happens in the Divine economy, but the damage is to your Spirit.

OUR SPIRITUAL ACCOUNT WILL NEVER KNOW SURPLUS

Nobel laureate and poet Rabindranath Tagore wrote, "Life is perpetually creative because it contains in itself that surplus which ever overflows the boundaries of the immediate time and space, restlessly pursuing its adventure of expression in the varied forms of self-realization."[5] This is so, but we cannot treat our spiritual lives like we can a savings or retirement account. We cannot save up God's gifts for a rainy day and not use them. Hoarding is not part of the Divine plan. The best we can do is to spend wisely and to always be creating more spiritual wealth for ourselves. Our spiritual retirement plan is already fully funded.

We must use the gifts we receive in a constant flow of compensation back to the Divine economy. We cannot save anything for the future, because we don't need to save Spirit and manifestation potential like we do money; there is a limitless supply for those who know how to tap into it. In fact, there is really no way to not spend the spiritual gifts that God brings into existence in our awareness, because they are dynamic and fluid. Wealth creates a reaction among people and businesses. New relationships grow and change on their own; they cannot be put into deep freeze. Work in the community breeds more work and more productivity. A new opportunity in business grows of its own accord as the creative power behind the business inspires others. Divine currency cannot stand still.

---

5. Rabindranath Tagore and Sisir Kumar Das, *A Miscellany* (New Delhi, India: Sahitya Akademi, 1996), 580.

GOD'S COLLECTION AGENCY

For years, American International Group, or AIG, was the largest insurance company in the world, worth hundreds of billions of dollars. As greed took control of the common sense of many financial professionals, this venerable company began making riskier and riskier decisions. Finally, they were in a position of spiritual default, not giving back to the community in equal measure the great wealth the community had given them. At this time, new financial minds came in and began pushing the company to sell credit default swaps, which are basically bets that a company will not default on its debts. AIG held hundreds of billions of credit default swaps, enough to ruin the company if all the bets came in. But that couldn't happen, could it?

When the economy collapsed, trillions in debt defaulted. Those bets came due. AIG nearly failed and had to take $175 billion in bailout money from the government. The financial minds at AIG hadn't given enough thought to the nature of the cosmos. They became severely indebted, forgetting that debt will be paid without exception. The cosmos will exact its price for what you have gained—and it doesn't ask you for permission.

We should watch for signs of change when we're at what seems like our greatest glory, because it could represent a sign that we're slipping into default. We may have time to even the balance.

ASSESS THE ABUNDANCE TREND IN YOUR LIFE

What happens in the material world when you default on multiple debt obligations? You cannot get a loan. You have not honored your trust deeds, so others will not trust you. That system functions in precisely the same way in manifestation from the Divine. The more you default on your obligations to God, the more meager will be your rewards for your manifestation.

In this way, even if you have an advanced ability to declare your I Am and use Divine Mind to bring into existence your desires, you will find yourself less and less able to do so. You become like a person who earns a great deal of money but who cannot get a mortgage because you have not paid your debts in the past. The Universe does not trust you with the fruits of manifestation because you will not pay the price in the form of growing, creating health and wealth for others, and fulfilling your role in God's purpose. You have a damaged cosmic credit rating, and you notice that no matter what you do, it becomes harder and harder to bring what you desire into your experience.

By doing an assessment of your abundance trend, you can see how well you have been paying back the obligations that God is always placing on your life. How have the blessings you have manifested through persistent thought increased or decreased in recent years? If you are seeing an increase, it is likely that you are meeting your obligations well and faithfully. If you are seeing a decrease, you are in danger of losing the trust of the manifestation engine, and you must find a solution.

The solution mirrors the solution in the earthly markets: credit repair. You must earn the trust of the Divine by repaying your obligation for even the smallest blessings and changing your orientation from inward-directed to outward-directed. When you can let go of ego and arrogance, embrace humility, and develop perspective, you can begin to repair your spiritual credit over time.

You may have noticed words I used over and over in this chapter: *perspective, humility, arrogance*. Following the Law of Debt requires you to always have perspective on your good fortune and to always be focused on projecting wealth, health, love, and opportunity outward while acknowledging that you are not their source.

WHAT WE HAVE LEARNED

- Debt, like compensation, works continuously behind the scenes, always exacting a price from you equal to the gifts you manifest.

- You have an obligation to repay debt by manifesting plenty, health, and wealth for others as well as ourselves.

- Arrogance and lack of perspective can lead us to lose sight of the Source of our well-being.

- Repeated defaults on our obligations can bring misfortune and damage your cosmic credit rating.

- Repaying debt to God increases your flow of abundance.

4

THE LAW OF DISCIPLINE

■ ■ ■ ■ ■

CORE PRINCIPLES

- The manifestation of prosperity occurs on God's time scale, not Man's.

- Actions that lead to short-term gain usually interfere with the manifestation of long-term riches.

- If a path to prosperity appears to be without sacrifice or discipline, it is false.

Right discipline consists not in external compulsion, but in the habits of mind which lead spontaneously to desirable rather than undesirable activities.

—Bertrand Russell, *On Education*

Recall the story of Jason Lester, who could have allowed the devastating paralysis of his arm to send him into a spiral of depression, anger, and desire for vengeance. Indeed, he did feel some of these emotions; who wouldn't? But his sense of discipline, instilled by his father during years of athletic training, was stronger. Lester returned to the baseball diamond and the football field. He began distance running and soon found that he had remarkable endurance. Though he could not use one arm, in 2003 he finished his first Ironman triathlon—a race in which one must swim, ride a bicycle, and run. In 2009, he became one of only twenty-three people to finish both the Hawaii and the Canada Ultraman races— double triathlons fit only for the world's elite extreme-distance athletes.

The key for this extraordinary man? Discipline. His motto has always been Never Stop. His training regimen is legendary, punishing, and brutal. He has admitted that what he does to his body to get ready for a race could be considered torture. But in order to pursue his greater purpose—racing, inspiring athletes, serving as a role model for other people with disabilities, and sharing his story about God's hand in his life—he has accepted the short-term discipline of putting one foot in front of the other, for as many as six hours daily, day after day.

Discipline is the subordination of short-term pleasure to long-term growth. If you are trying to lose pounds, then giving in to short-term pleasure means you surrender to the temptation to eat the piece of chocolate cake. But if you do, you short circuit one of the small gains upon which long-term triumph is built. Achieving any great purpose in one's life is never a matter of a single world-changing victory; it is a matter of small steps taken each day, adding up over time to transformative change. A novel is written one word at a time, a few pages every day. A person loses thirty pounds by eating a little less and moving a little more, dropping a pound per week. We save money for retirement by putting away a few dollars a week—an insignificant amount until thirty years of compound interest pass.

Discipline divorced from wisdom is not true discipline, but merely the meaningless following of custom, which is only a disguise for stupidity.
—Rabindranath Tagore, *A Miscellany*

REJECTING TRENDS AND SHALLOW DESIRES

The manifestation of prosperity works in the same way, but it is easy to become sidetracked by the allure of the short-term. If you ask financial professionals, they will tell you that leaving your money in a diversified stock portfolio will produce better returns for your 401(k) over the long-term. You should not bail out of the market when it dives, they insist. Yet what do many of us do? We chase the glamour stock, and we get out of the market when it's at its bottom. We let short-term thinking hinder our long-term discipline and are the poorer for it.

Bringing true wealth—a blend of financial security, ongoing economic opportunity, personal wellness, mental health, strong relationships, and spiritual enlightenment—into your corporeal experience demands discipline. Remember that sending a personal I Am declaration of your prosperity message into the Universe is not like pulling up to the drive-through window at a cosmic fast-food restaurant; you cannot simply ask and receive. God's system is far too wisely designed for that. It is built to reward those who go beyond the simple asking and instead exhibit the steady focus on doing what is right rather than what is easy or instantly rewarding. Maintaining mental focus on your prosperity goal, disciplining your thoughts to dwell only on the achievement of your purpose, giving to others and the cosmos to clear space for the gifts to come—these all must be done with consistency in order for spiritual prosperity to manifest as physical wealth and happiness.

THE LAW OF DISCIPLINE

Realizing God's prosperity demands a rejection of short-term, easy satisfactions and a long-term focus on doing right, maintaining consistency of thought, and becoming the wealth one wishes to receive.

When a path to prosperity appears before you that seems easy and requires little or no sacrifice or spiritual development on your part, it is virtually certain to be an illusory path that leads to nothing but frustration, wasted effort, and disappointment. The disciplined mind is the gateway to the abundance granted to us by God's economic system.

The reason the Law of Discipline exists is not because God demands some sort of proof of your faith or fitness to inherit his kingdom. It exists because the wealth that you manifest in your physical experience is not simply a new car, a new house, or a fatter bank account. That is the outward form of an inward transformation. The truth of the matter is that the wealth of this world brought to you by the declaration of your I Am intention will always be a reflection of the being you are in the process of becoming as that wealth begins to manifest. You must become the characteristics of the prosperity that you wish to experience in order for that prosperity to press out of the ether.

BECOMING PROSPERITY

What do I mean by this? Let me illustrate with a story. In the nineteenth century, two brothers inherited an Alaskan gold claim from their father, a claim he said on his deathbed would make them rich beyond their wildest dreams. The only thing was, the claim was located in a remote part of the Alaska territory that would be difficult and dangerous to reach. It would take each brother's total commitment to reach the land and turn the claim into the promised fortune. The father, wishing not to simply pass along unearned wealth to his sons and damage their character, made the following stipulation in his will: To claim the gold, each son had to reach the physical site of the gold deposit within ninety days of the old man's death. If either son failed in this, he would lose his right to the fortune.

Both brothers equipped themselves for a long, arduous journey through the mountains and set out. Initially, they traveled together, but early in the journey, the younger brother began to show a tendency to turn aside and be slothful. He would linger by lakes and fish, pan for gold in streams, and ask his older brother to carry his pack over the steepest parts of the trail. At first, his older brother was reluctant to leave and stayed with him during these delays. But eventually, the elder brother pushed on, warning his younger sibling that if he did not dedicate himself to the trail, he would never reach the destination. Scoffing, the younger brother told his elder that he would not only reach the site of the gold claim but be there before the older brother. Shaking his head, the elder moved on.

His road was hard and covered many miles. Each day, the steep trails exhausted him. But over time, as he devoted his full attention to walking the many miles, he became fitter and stronger and more able to walk long distances. Finally, after two months and more than eight hundred miles, the older brother reached the gold claim, knelt, and gave thanks to God and his father. At the site he found documents ready for his signature. He signed and began the task of extracting the gold ore from the ground.

Far behind, his younger brother continued to dawdle and delay. Finally, realizing he was in danger of losing his inheritance, the younger sibling took to the trail with a vengeance. But he had not spent enough time dedicated to walking the great distance; he lacked the endurance to travel the miles and climb the endless hills. In the end, when it appeared that he would not make it to the claim site in time, he took a shortcut out of desperation, vanished into the woods, and was never seen again. No one knows what became of him.

This story illustrates the central principle behind the Law of Discipline. Only by undergoing a personal transformation on the way to manifesting the prosperity we desire do we become fit to claim that prosperity and realize it to the fullest. When I say that we must become the characteristics of the prosperity to which we aspire, these are the characteristics I refer to:

- Steady focus on your goals
- Adherence to the central principles of your character
- Diligence
- Generosity
- Justice
- Humility
- Positive thought
- Regular practice of meditation or prayer

THE PRICE OF PLENTY

When you orient your Divine Mind on the manifestation of a certain type of prosperity from the invisible substance of the cosmos, the process does not end there. It only begins. The universe is not an order-and-forget-it machine that simply sends you what you want at the push of a button. It is a mirror that reflects who you are in the act of becoming and brings forth a prosperity result in concordance with the discipline that you exhibit while your thought is taking form.

So when you think prosperity into your life, the result of that process will directly reflect the discipline you show after your thoughts initially project into the spiritual plane. Do you continue to maintain your thought on the achievement of plenty and abundance, refusing to allow defeatist thinking to pollute your Mind? Do you continue to work to your best ability at what you do without worry for the results? Do you maintain your intention that your coming prosperity will be applied for the greater good of many rather than only for yourself? Do you carry on with assisting others, acting with honor and rejecting relationships with people who do not do so? All these choices are wealth producing because they color the type of prosperity the cosmos will bring forth into your corporeal world. The more diligent you are in your work, the more generous your Spirit is, the more humble you are in the face of God, and the greater your prosperity will be in all areas.

For example, let us use the situation so many people find themselves in now, that of seeking work. Let's say that you are working at a job that barely covers your bills and leaves you very vulnerable. You declare one day, strong in your Divine Mind, that "I Am a new career of great opportunity and will manifest that opportunity in my life." That is an excellent start, but the discipline you show following the statement of that intention will determine how it plays out. Sadly, you immediately start to sabotage your own intention:

- You begin to doubt that your I Am will come to pass.
- You begin to slack off at your current job in anticipation of the new career to come.
- You buy new things on credit, figuring that your coming good fortune will pay for them.
- You become impatient and figure that the Universe owes you, an arrogant position that leads you to take shortcuts to supposed wealth, such as gambling.

In the end, how would your aspired-to prosperity come to pass? You discover that a desirable new position is opening at your current place of employment, and you would surely have been chosen for it, but because your recent performance has been so erratic and your attitude so off-putting, someone else gets the job. Instead, you receive a small cost-of-living raise that leaves you no better off than you were before. Your prosperity has arrived, but in a form that was sabotaged by your lack of discipline. What arrived in your experience reflected the person you were becoming while you were waiting for it to manifest—slothful, proud, wasteful, and lacking in faith.

Discipline is the price of all long-term good things: health, a slender body, a strong retirement, a good education, a prosperous future. You cannot hope to manifest what you deserve—what God has ordained for you to have in his system—without adhering to discipline.

The need for discipline is reflected in the events that have taken place during the recession. As people have lost fortunes and found themselves sinking into financial ruin, it has become clear that activities and choices that served the short-term, ego-driven desire to have and accrue more for its own sake were destined to result in great loss and agony. The couple who refinanced a home multiple times at the top of the market in favor of purchasing more material possessions? They are now in foreclosure and bankruptcy. The investor who bought into trendy stocks when the Dow was at its peak? That investor has seen his shares' value drop to practically nothing.

On the other hand, the couple who shepherded their family through the hard times with steady savings and values of service, thrift, and generosity to others always first—that couple is doing just fine. Even if times become hard, your generosity means that you have created a conduit of potential aid that will come to you through the goodwill of others. Discipline produces results in line with the quality of your character and the maturity of your choices.

ONCE PROSPERITY MANIFESTS, DISCIPLINE REMAINS NECESSARY

It is tempting for us to assume that once the prosperity we desire has appeared in our lives via the conduit of our Divine Mind we can become consumed by it, abandon our disciplined ways, and that this will not matter. But nothing could be further from the truth. In fact, the act of personal transformation and the act of Divine manifestation are the same: both evolutionary processes that have no stopping point. Because prosperity is a process of becoming, not a delivery system that simply drops wealth on your doorstep and leaves, you must continue to exercise personal discipline in order to keep what you have gained.

How often have we seen lottery winners embody this truth? You'll see some lucky, downtrodden soul hold up a winning lottery ticket and walk away with $20 million. This individual is set for life, right? Wrong. Far more often than you would believe, such windfalls lead to even more troubles. The fact is, more than 60 percent of lottery winners declare personal bankruptcy within five years of their win. Why? Two reasons. First, their great gain did not come as a result of any sort of mental or spiritual pact with the Universe and God's system. No personal virtue and steadfastness won them their money, so any terrible habits they had before becoming rich—debt accumulation, drug abuse, laziness—persisted afterward.

Second, wealth is a magnifier of our personal virtues and faults. The generous man with abundant material riches will become more generous. The envious man with wealth will become more poisonously envious. So when lottery winners who know nothing of the Divine Mind and discipline come into unearned wealth, their faults boom and blossom like monsters in a Japanese movie. This is why so often you will read of lottery winners who end up in court, destitute, after blowing their windfalls on gambling, drugs, and other poor choices. Wealth does not change who we are; it clarifies who we are. We must become richer in order to both obtain and keep riches.

DISCIPLINE MEANS DELAYING GRATIFICATION

They say that maturity is, in part, the time when a person gains the power to delay his or her own gratification to serve a long-term good. This explains in part why teenagers think only of the now and cannot resist short-term pleasures: their brains simply are wired that way. That is God's order of things, and it certainly produces the life lessons that can lead to greater wisdom as the years pass. But when we are in the fullness of our maturity, it is essential that we come to a place where we view discipline and the delay of gratification as its own reward. Our maturity must be, in some part, our satisfaction as we do what is right rather than what is easy.

The point in delaying gratification is quite simple: we do not know how much time must pass before we realize the fruits of the I Am intention we send into the world of Spirit. It might be a matter of days before the object of our prosperity desire begins to show itself; alternatively, it might be years. We simply do not know, and it is not our place to know. God himself may not even know; he has set up the mechanism by which our desires are made manifest in accordance with his laws, but that does not mean he will control how the mechanism operates. That would violate the free will we must wield to control our destinies.

So since we do not know how or when our prosperity desire will come to pass, there is great danger in letting ourselves be tempted off the path of the focused mind and diligence that produces blessings. If your Divine Mind has stated that you are and shall experience a fine mansion in your life, it could take two years for all the cosmic tumblers to click into place and bring you and that house into corporeal harmony. But if, in the meantime, you decide you cannot wait for that house and instead buy a car, what will happen? Your mind will veer off the path of focus on what you wished to manifest and toward that car. You will lose discipline and your long-term manifestation may never come to pass.

Gratification of our desires before their time bears another peril: the potential that we may not have developed the depth of character to deal with the challenges presented by great opportunity. Look at many of the people who have become instant celebrities via reality television. They frequently self-destruct because they abandon the character qualities that made them good individuals before fame arrived and give themselves over entirely to short-term gratification: parties, selling out their principles, substance abuse, infidelity, and so on. If prosperity arrives before you are ready, it could become more curse than blessing.

RITUAL PROVIDES INVALUABLE SUPPORT FOR DISCIPLINE

Rabindranath Tagore wrote, "For the current of our spiritual life, creeds and rituals are channels that may thwart or help according to their fixity or openness. When a symbol or spiritual idea becomes rigidly elaborate in its construction, it supplants the idea which it should support."[1] Ritual is second nature to the followers of any creed, whose necessary expression takes the form of repetitive and meditative actions, whether they be the Christian taking communion, the Muslim making the pilgrimage to Mecca, or the Hindu reciting the ancient passages of the Rig Veda.

According to the Eastern spiritual tradition known as Vedanta, all spiritual traditions represent different aspects of the same path to God. There is little doubt that the rituals inherent to each religion form a continuum of repetition that leads to worthwhile action: self-discipline, mental strengthening, meditative adeptness.

Ritual is vital to the Law of Discipline, because it is through ritualized activity that we find the simplest path to ignoring short-term gratification in favor of staying on the long-term path of growth. If

---

1. Ibid., 51.

you are trying to get in excellent physical condition, the surest path to success comes if you rise at the same time each morning and work out at the same time. The ritual repetition of such activity becomes comforting and predictable, making work and sacrifice not only palatable but satisfying. The same is true for finance: sending a check to your retirement account like clockwork at the beginning of each month will slowly, over time, serve your purpose of creating long-term prosperity.

How can you ritualize your growth during the period in which your manifestation is invisibly taking shape? How can you put systems and boundaries into place that will enable you to keep your eyes looking forward and keep you oriented on character, growth, and strength?

IT IS POSSIBLE TO BE TOO DISCIPLINED

It would seem that discipline can never come but to be of benefit. However, it is not as simple as that. A story from ancient times explains why. A hermitic monk was determined to gain ultimate wisdom by forsaking the things of the body, all material comforts, save clothing and enough water to stave off death. So he secreted himself in a cave far from humanity and began to meditate on the great matters of the world. He did not eat except at the utmost extremity, and he did not drink save when his mouth was parched and his consciousness about to desert him.

Years of this deprivation passed, until finally the monk had realized his great wisdom: the secrets of life, death, and fate. Not long after this, several pilgrims on the trail to Jerusalem came upon his cave and were astonished to find this wizened man whose eyes yet gleamed fierce knowledge. They asked him, "Can you share with us the knowledge of the ages, brother?" The old monk opened his mouth to speak ... and no sound issued. He tried to write his wisdom, but he had forgotten how to write. And so he possessed the secrets of God but had no way to express them to others. His excessive deprivation, masquerading as discipline, had robbed him of the full fruits of his personal sacrifice.

In the context of manifesting prosperity, what does this mean? It means that it is possible to be too unforgiving of yourself—so unforgiving in the interest of being studious and holy that you cease to see yourself as worthy of prosperity. In doing so, you shatter the riches that may otherwise have come your way. For you must see yourself not only as being that which you desire but as deserving of that which you desire. If false discipline breeds self-hatred or intolerance for your own weaknesses, the mind can turn to negative, defeatist thinking, which kills prosperity before it can even be born.

DISCIPLINE INVOLVES SACRIFICE

We live in an entitlement society, and that is a dangerous thing. When we begin to feel that we are entitled to something, we lose sight of the qualities that inspire others to help us achieve our goals: spiritual strength, wisdom, confidence, compassion. But in reality, we are entitled only to that which our Divine Mind earns for us through the expansion of our awareness, our relentless focus on manifestation, and our determination to become that which we seek. Woven into that reality is the necessity of sacrifice: we must sacrifice easy pleasures in order to experience greater gains.

Nowhere is this more visible to the average person than in the process by which we buy a home. Left to our own devices, would we not frequently give in to the temptation to spend $1,000 per month or more on pleasures like food, wine, and gambling? But because our contract with a lender requires it, we must sacrifice those pleasures, which would only trip us up in the long run, and make our monthly mortgage payment. Over the short-term, we may regret not having the money to spend; in the long-term, we benefit from the sacrifice and enforced discipline when we make the final payment and own our house.

In the context of the Law of Discipline, sacrifice is a simple commandment: be prepared to surrender any patterns of thought or action that prevailed prior to the time you made your I Am declaration. Let them fade and adopt a new mode of being if you hope to realize what you intend.

MAINTAINING DISCIPLINE IN CHALLENGING TIMES

Discipline is a hard commodity to come by during times of easy money and little work. It is easy for us to delude ourselves into thinking that riches, renown, and opportunity that come to us during such times are the products of our diligence, wisdom, and inherent self-worth. In reality, they are chimeras, false images that lure us away from the probity and personal growth that lead to lasting wealth and well-being.

This is why part of the act and attitude of discipline also entails maintaining your perspective when times are good and the bank account is flush. Without discipline of mind and emotions, it is possible to become carried away with the idea that good fortune is deserved and earned, when in fact it is a matter of accident—a lottery win that reflects nothing about the worthiness of the recipient.

To be disciplined, practice staying in a calm, nonanticipatory state of mind no matter what comes your way—good fortune or ill. Remaining detached from the ups and downs of an individual day or week will help you maintain the long-term suppleness of Mind to focus on what you wish to manifest for life, the only span of time that truly matters.

WHAT WE HAVE LEARNED

- Discipline brings out the qualities that determine the scope and kind of the wealth your Mind can produce.

- The cosmic economy is a reflection of your qualities— laudable and otherwise.

- Discipline demands long-term thinking and the rejection of easy gain.

- Once you achieve your desire, discipline is still necessary to keep it.

- Discipline also means not getting too high or too low over life's trials.

5

THE LAW OF DIVINE PURPOSE

■　■　■　■　■

CORE PRINCIPLES

- God has a purpose for all the prosperity that you might realize.

- The ease with which you can generate prosperity with your Mind is a gauge of how in-line you are with God's purpose for you.

- If you wish to find more wealth and retain what you have, you must fine-tune your purpose.

I am here for a purpose and that purpose is to grow into a mountain, not to shrink to a grain of sand. Henceforth will I apply all my efforts to become the highest mountain of all and I will strain my potential until it cries for mercy.

—Og Mandino, *The Greatest Secret in the World*

No doubt during this period of massive economic upheaval, we have all heard stories of the rich losing all they have. In fact, as this book was being written, research appeared in the *New York Times* saying that the superrich were losing their wealth faster than any other group.[1] While the idea of someone worth $100 million one day and only $10 million the next may provoke some eye rolling, pay less attention to the loss of wealth and more to the reasons behind it. Then you will begin to understand Divine Purpose.

It is virtually certain that the majority of wealthy individuals who lost much or all of their wealth did so because they were not applying it to the purpose that God had ordained for them. God's economic system is a conscious system, not a mere collection of spiritual machinery that spits out prosperity to those who ask for it. There is intent behind the manifestation of a desired prosperous outcome in any person's life—a requirement set forth by the cosmos that the recipient of the gift act according to that requirement and use that which is received in a way that serves the larger purpose set down by God for that person. In

---

1. David Leonhardt and Geraldine Fabrikant, "Rise of the Superrich Hits a Sobering Wall," *New York Times*, August 21, 2009; http://www.nytimes.com/2009/08/21/business/economy/21inequality.html.

other words, God's intelligent, aware system delivers wealth to the Mind that knows how to manifest it—but there are strings attached.

Author John R. Noe said, "Purpose is the engine, the power that drives and directs our lives."[2] In the arena of wealth that we bring into our experience using the power of the I Am intention and the mentality of experiencing that which we desire already made manifest, Divine Purpose is like a binding agent that lends our prosperity permanence. Any prosperity realized by humanity is like a temperamental plant in a garden; if it is tended and fed properly, it will take root and endure for many years. But if it is neglected, it will wither and die long before its appointed life span. Wealth as granted through God's system must be used (at least in part) to serve the individual, unique purpose designated for the individual who receives it. If it is not, the wealth is impermanent. It will rot and cannot last.

We see this in our society continually in these days of fear, displacement, and financial chaos. When an individual is aware of God's intended purpose for his prosperity and dutifully proclaims and acts upon that purpose, he can be buffeted by harsh times but there is always solace, support, and protection. A case from the news illustrates this: A couple in Denver, Colorado, had an idea back in 2006 to start a restaurant that would serve the growing population of working poor and homeless in their area. Fortunate enough to have the capital to start this enterprise and blessed with divine inspiration, they launched SAME (So All May Eat) Café in 2007. The concept is simple: no prices. You order your food and afterward, you pay what you think the meal was worth. If you can't afford anything, you help out in the café for an hour.

---

2. John R. Noe, *Peale Performance Principles for High Achievers* (Hollywood, FL: Federick Fell Publishers, 2006), 105.

A recipe for retail disaster, right? Wrong. SAME has thrived, serving more than fifteen thousand customers a year and providing a place for street folk to get hot, healthy, organic food that's not a handout but a gesture of respect: we feed you, you pitch in. The restaurant wastes almost nothing and has done so well that the founders are getting offers to franchise the concept around the country.

This uplifting tale is balanced, sadly, by stories about those who ignored God's call when they achieved their wealth and did nothing to serve his purpose. We have seen it in the headlines: scandals, lawsuits, fraud charges, mansions put on the auction block, and so on. When we take a closer look at the individuals behind these fiscal debacles, we often see people whose wealth was used only to serve themselves. God did not enter into the discussion. By not watering the roots of their prosperity, they allowed it to wither and die as soon as the rains of the economic bubble stopped falling.

WEALTH COMES WHEN PURPOSE GROWS

Proverbs 24:3–4 reads, "Through wisdom is a house built; and by understanding it is established. And by knowledge shall the chambers be filled with all precious and pleasant riches." The acquisition of lasting wealth is brought about by the knowledge and understanding of God's purpose for the wealth, for there is no wealth without purpose.

THE LAW OF DIVINE PURPOSE

If you do not have the prosperity and wealth to which you aspire, it is probably because you are serving your own purpose, not God's, with the wealth that you have.

This Law functions in one of two ways. In one, people can possess wealth, and the permanence of that wealth will be determined by the faithfulness with which they devote some of it to serving the purpose brought to them by Spirit. In the other, people who cannot seem to experience greater wealth turn out to be repelling further prosperity because they are using only their current wealth to serve selfish needs with no thought of God's plan. In either case, ignoring Divine Purpose and using prosperity exclusively for self-directed goals act to sabotage the existence of that wealth in the future; either it departs or it does not come in the first place. In other words, if you wish to realize lifelong prosperity, you must know and serve God's purpose with a large share of your prosperity. As Proverbs 13:11 states, "Dishonest money dwindles away, but he who gathers money little by little makes it grow."

This does not mean that you must engage in charity or turn your fine home into a shelter for the homeless; generous deeds are not automatically in tune with the purpose God has in mind for you. The stereotype that all Divine deeds must involve selfless giving and charity without reward is delusion. The truth is that many kinds of deeds serve Divine Purpose. Some may indeed be altruistic and charitable, while others may involve entrepreneurship and creating jobs, running for political office, engaging in ascetic spiritual study, building a facility for people in your community, or even writing books or music that inspire others. There are many ways to serve God with wealth.

How to Know Your Purpose

Given this revelation, the obvious questions are, how do you discover God's purpose for you, and how do you know that you are following it? The answer to the first question is surprisingly simple: follow your passion. Each of us is imbued at creation with one or more pure, fiery passions—desires to follow a path that may have nothing to do with what our families wish for us or what we want to do in order to make a certain amount of money. These passions are often buried, but they cannot be silenced. They well up within us throughout our lives, immortal and impossible to ignore. The reason for this is that passion is God's purpose singing within us.

> *A true desire is not to have but to be. We are whole creatures in potential, and the true purpose of desire is to unfold that wholeness, to become what we can be. As Goethe says, "Desire is the presentiment of our inner abilities, and the forerunner of our ultimate accomplishments."*
> —Eric Butterworth, *Spiritual Economic*

Thus it is that young men who are expected to become lawyers, following in the footsteps of their fathers and grandfathers, defy family and tradition to follow their passions and become shipwrights, cellists, or Peace Corps volunteers. Essayist William Hazlitt said, "A strong passion for any object will ensure success, for the desire of the end will point out the means."[3] Passion drives us to face any obstacle, upend the previous structure of our lives, and endure years of hardship in order to do what we felt we are meant to do.

Where do you think such overpowering desire comes from? It can only come from one source: the Spirit of God burning in us. God created our spirits with a purpose in mind, each a small piece in the great puzzle of evolving human existence. God cannot act in the physical world, being pure Spirit; we are each his proxies. Each of us plays an infinitesimal but vital role in the physical realization

3. William Hazlitt, *The Round Table* (London: Scribner & Welford, 1869), 48.

of God's spiritual plan; no one is insignificant. Even the smallest bolt in a great suspension bridge may cause disaster if it fails—and so, each man and woman has a vital purpose. When we listen to and obey that passion that speaks to us in the middle of the night and calls to us to do things that may seem insane by the light of the day, we are truly in the center of Divine Purpose.

Now, passion does not always ask us to do things that destroy what we have built, such as selling a successful business in order to pursue a life of impoverished preaching. Sometimes, the price will be this high; other times, it will be much lower. Purpose and passion are different for each individual. But they have one essential factor in common, something all of us must remember: *God will always call you to a purpose whose primary function is to inspire others to evolve spiritually and find the Divine in themselves.*

In following chapters, this is staggeringly important. All passion placed in us by God is designed to guide us toward decisions and pursuits that ultimately help our fellow travelers discover their own passions and their own Divine Minds. This is why Divine Purpose can take so many different forms. For some individuals, it may be pure giving and devotion to helping the downtrodden, but in others it might be working to preserve nature, play a sport, or launch a business. But in the wholeness of God's vision (which is impossible for us to perceive in its entirety), each activity born of pure passion serves a goal: inspiring those who witness it to grow in Spirit and take their own places in God's purpose.

So when you hear God's voice speaking to you in a passion that gnaws at your soul, listen. Do not deny. Passion left unattended blights life and happiness, leaving us empty and hollow. Instead, realize that when you are living your passion, wealth will come to you in order that you may better inspire others to discover and pursue their own passions.

The second question—about knowing if you are in the center of God's purpose for you—finds answers from a careful and honest observation of your life and fortunes. Adherence to purpose is a self-fulfilling machine of manifestation: if you are in line with Divine Purpose with whatever prosperity you possess, you will find that your I Am desire for greater prosperity increases your wealth. But if you are ignoring your passion, and thus God's purpose, then you will not only find that new wealth is impossible to come by, but the wealth you have seems to be slipping away.

The corrective power of coming into coherence with Divine Purpose can be seen in this story, which perhaps reflects the maxim, "If you want to keep something, give it away." A Wall Street banker who made a fortune at the height of the bull market and real estate bubble was worried that his wealth was built on a foundation of nothing more than hype. Furthermore, he feared that if his bank began to lose more money, he would lose his job and everything he had built.

Indeed, it began to look like this was the case. His company foundered, his stocks fell, and his debts began to come due. It appeared as though he would be on the chopping block and bound for financial ruin. But one night, he decided that before he lost all his money, he would do something he had always wanted to do: give to people who needed it more than he did. So he took $5,000 from his bank account, went to the poorest section of his city, and gave the money to the owners of a small neighborhood store that was the source of jobs, groceries, and hope for the area's down-and-out residents. The next day he did the same thing, and the next.

A week later, his superiors called him into their offices. He assumed he was going to receive the news that he had been laid off. Instead, his bosses informed him that they had heard about his actions via a local news program and that he was the kind of person they wanted to lead the bank going forward. Instead of being laid off, he received a promotion. His passionate actions to aid others stopped a life of selfishness and resulted in a new destiny.

PURSUING WEALTH FOR ITS OWN SAKE SABOTAGES WEALTH

In a study conducted in 1960, fifteen hundred business-school graduates were asked what they wanted to pursue first after gradation, money or mission. Category A consisted of those graduates who wanted to make money first, so they could do what they wanted later. Eighty-seven percent of the graduates fell into this category. They fell victim to the grand delusion: "I'm going to sacrifice my family now to be with them later." They had limited vision and paid no attention to the God-created passion inside them.

Category B comprised those who were going to pursue passion first, confident in the fact that money would follow. Only 17 percent of the graduates, just 255 people, fell into this group. By 1980, there were 101 millionaires in the overall group of fifteen hundred. Only one was from Category A. The other one hundred were from Category B. The author of the study concluded that the overwhelming majority of rich people became so by doing work that they found profoundly absorbing. They intended to follow their passion and make a difference. They chose to make a difference over making money, and in the end they accomplished both.

Not much more needs to be said. If you pursue wealth for its own sake, you may achieve it for a time, but it will be transitory. Only if you pursue passion in the service of God's purpose will you (a) find the inspiration to work the hours necessary to achieve prosperity, and (b) inspire others to aid you on your journey.

Divine Purpose Does Not Mean Surrendering All Wealth to God's Purpose

Contrary to what some misguided religious leaders may try to tell you, God does not want us to take vows of poverty. In fact, God wants you to be rich. He wants you to live in a mansion—but according to his condition, which is that you will use your prosperity to serve his greater purpose. That does not mean you must give all your money to charity and leave nothing with which to meet your financial obligations. It simply means that some of what you are lucky enough to have should go toward serving the passion that you feel in the depths of your soul.

This does not just apply to grand gestures by millionaires. Far from it. God works his wonders in the hearts and hands of the meek and small just as much as he does through the rich and great. As Paul wrote in Philippians 4:12–13,

I know what it is to be in need, and I know what it is to have plenty. I have learned the secret of being content in any and every situation, whether well fed or hungry, whether living in plenty or in want. I can do everything through him who gives me strength.

A woman who owns a modest home and has a passion for knitting decided that God wanted her to knit and teach other women to do the same. She followed this call in her heart and her effort taught dozens of women young and old this ancient art, and they began sending handmade knitted goods to children in Afghanistan and to premature babies in American hospitals.

Doubtless this passion-born enterprise will continue to reward the woman in many ways, as it will the expanding family of people who come together in love, watch out for each other, and protect each other during hard times. This venture did not require much of the woman's modest wealth, just her time and the use of her home. Yet she achieved wonders. That is truly being in line with God's purpose.

EGO IS THE VILLAIN THAT CORRUPTS WEALTH

This goes back to an idea we have touched upon before: when we begin to believe that our brains, hard work, or virtues are the source of prosperity, we take the first steps down the road to losing it all. The truth is that everything we have is on loan from God and comes to us through his system; we have nothing that is permanently ours, save our Spirits. We came to this world with nothing and will leave with nothing.

However, the people who are the self-styled "kings of the world" can easily delude themselves into thinking that they are the sole source of their wealth and power. The danger in thinking this way is that it blinds us to the need to use our wealth to serve God's purpose. If we believe the propaganda that all we have is due to our own inherent wonderfulness, then are we not more likely to jealously guard it and hoard it, thinking that giving anything away is also giving away our status and worth? This leads to willful rejection of passion and a refusal to participate in anything that does not further our narrow perception of wealth. Wealth becomes everything and eventually it vanishes.

On the other hand, when we reject ego and think of all that we have as being on temporary loan, like a cosmic library book, from God, we become freer and more generous. What we have was never really ours to begin with; we were merely stewards chosen to share God's bounty with the less enlightened and thereby help them become more enlightened. You can see how this perspective would surely foster greater generosity, cooperation, creativity, and joy—as well as ensure that the flow of prosperity into your life continues unabated.

It Is Not Possible to Dedicate Too Much Prosperity

You cannot overcommit your prosperity to the true works of God. It is simply not possible. When you are working in the Spirit and centered in a passion that is truly born of God, then no matter how great a quantity of your money, time, or knowledge you give away to others, more will flow into your hands as a result. It is impossible to become impoverished when you depend on God as your sole means of support.

There is a purity to the Divine Purpose of God that waxes in our lives as we come to rely more on Spirit and less on money or any other earthly, material means of subsistence. This is why ministers will tell people to give much of what they have to others if they want to experience blessings beyond measure. Creating space in your life, truly following your passion, and depending only on the Lord to hold you up provokes marvelous results from the Universe.

One of the best examples of this principle comes from a story from several years ago about a middle-aged man who left his work in the medical field because he felt called to create and build musical instruments: guitars, drums, harps, flutes, and so on. When he would play these instruments in his neighborhood, the people flocked to him, especially those living on the street. Eventually, he began making instruments for homeless men and women and giving them away, and after a while this took up all his time. He was not selling any instruments or making any money, and he went into arrears on his mortgage. But being a God-fearing man, he believed that if he kept to what he knew was his ordained purpose, God would provide.

Time passed and he went into foreclosure. The day of the foreclosure auction, the man still insisted that God would provide, though he was beginning to doubt. Then, minutes before the auction was to begin, the crowd before his house was parted by a group of more than forty street people, all carrying instruments the man had made. The leader of the group stood up and explained what the man's instruments had meant to people who usually went unseen, and told the crowd that the homeless had come to play a concert on the man's front lawn as a way of saying thanks. They hadn't known that a foreclosure auction would be taking place, and the man wondered if they could play anyway.

The group agreed and began playing jazz, blues, and classical music—not well, but with passion. After an hour, the assembled would-be buyers of the man's house were so moved by this tribute that they actually collected enough money for the man to not only bring his mortgage current but pay off the balance. It's an astonishing tale of reliance on God and pure passion.

This is another law where observation of what is going on in your life will yield valuable information. Look at how prosperity has come to you in the past. If it has not come easily, could it be because you are ignoring your Divine Purpose? Look at the history of "easy come, easy go" as it may have played out in your life. If you seem to come into wealth only to have it slip through your fingers quickly, you may be devoting your time and attention to things that are about your own ego rather than the passion that serves God. Be vigilant about your choices and try to open yourself to the passions within.

What We Have Learned

- God wants you to be wealthy.

- You will know your purpose in the unquenchable passion God has placed within you.

- The purpose of Divinely ordained passion is to inspire others to grow into God's purpose.

- Pursuing passion is the surest way to find wealth.

- Ego blinds you to the need to serve a higher purpose because wealth becomes the source of your self-worth.

6

THE LAW OF
EMPLOYMENT

■ ■ ■ ■ ■

CORE PRINCIPLES

- Mental and spiritual activity is the default position of the universe.

- God wishes you to have gainful employment.

- The outcome of all Divine employment will be spiritual growth and enlightenment.

The crowning fortune of a man is to be born to some pursuit which finds him employment and happiness, whether it be to make baskets, or broad swords, or canals, or statues, or songs.

—Ralph Waldo Emerson, *Conduct of Life*

Employment is on everyone's mind as we weather the severe storms of economic chaos and fear. Perhaps more than any other factor, lack of employment defines the frightening times we've had. Lost jobs weigh down the economy, cripple chances for recovery, result in bankruptcies and foreclosures, and perhaps worst of all, harm the Spirit of those people who have lost their jobs and spent endless hours, days, and months searching for employment. Look at the faces of those who cannot seem to find a new job no matter what they do: hopeless, exhausted, confused.

There are many good reasons for this. In great measure our work defines who we are; when someone we meet at a social event wants to learn more about us, he asks what we do. When we cannot find work, our identity suffers. Our sense of purpose is lost, and we are rudderless. But have you ever wondered why this should be? In a culture that seems to prize leisure just as highly as work, why are we so compelled to work? Why is it so vital, not just to our debtors and our future retirement, that we hold down a job and spend our days productively?

The underlying reason is that God designed the cosmos to be in motion, employed and active. All things have their roles to play;

nothing in the universe is static or purposeless. We are meant to be employed and designed to be shaping the world—actively participating in its evolution. This is why lack of employment seems so jarring, so harmful to our well-being: it's not how we were meant to function. Lack of employment strips the Spirit of meaning and leaves the Divine Mind with no focus and no sense of accomplishment.

THE SEARCH FOR EMPLOYMENT

The desperate human need for employment is driven by the need for money, of course. But it's also driven by our innate desire to be in harmony with God's order—even if many times we do not understand that desire or even acknowledge it. Combine financial desperation with Divine passion and you can get some gut-wrenching tales about the search for work, especially in a down economy.

Take the story of the woman who was offered a new job as an administrative assistant and gave notice at her old job, only to find that the new job offer had been rescinded, leaving her with nothing. She was then forced to crawl back to her former employer and beg for her old job.

Then there was the gentleman who interviewed for an executive position at an international manufacturing company and was very excited about the job until the interviewer asked if his wife would be traveling with him internationally. When he said no, she had her own career, the interviewer inquired if the man would be willing to travel with a female "escort." End of interview.

And finally there was the man who, in an act that must be filed under the heading "pouring salt in the wound," received a rejection letter from the company he'd interviewed with . . . postage due.

When we are cast adrift by the economic situation, the troubles of our employer, or our own inability to perform on the job, we can become desperate. That inborn need to tune our lives to the pitch ordained by God can compel us to take drastic action and tolerate conditions we would normally reject in order to find employment and feel in harmony with the Lord again.

THE LAW OF EMPLOYMENT

God built the mechanism of the cosmos so that all things, including us, must have activity and purpose. You were meant to be employed and serving as custodian of the world's evolution.

Each of us is meant to be employed and to play a role in the complex ticking of the cosmic clockwork. There are many reasons employment is so critical to the balance and function of our physical existence. The following are the reasons behind why we work.

POSSESSING AN IDEA OF WORTH

Work produces money, and money is the agent of change. Robert Collier said, "All riches have their origin in mind. Wealth is in ideas—not money."[1] That may seem to contradict the facts about money, but it does not. Money is an idea. Think about it: what is the inherent worth of money? It has none. It only has worth because humankind has agreed upon the idea that money can be used to move people and objects. Money stems from the Mind of Man, and since the Mind of Man has its origins in the Mind of God, money is actually an idea from the Mind of God!

---

1. Robert Collier, *The Secret of the Ages* (Radford, VA: Wilder Publication, 2008), 64.

The way to earn money is to work, that much is clear. But the purpose of earning money is not simply to pay your bills. There are many ways to live, and if you chose to, you could live roughly and simply and probably not have to work. But that would defy God's desire, and this is why: money is the agent of change in the world. Money motivates and moves and provokes action and brings about many of the desires that we bring forth when we manifest our I Am intentions. When you earn money, you do more than settle debts, save for the future, and perhaps invest; you spread the powerful idea of change throughout human society. Through your spending and investing, that power gets into the hands of others—entrepreneurs, artists, builders—who in turn use the idea of money to fulfill their small part of God's Divine intention. Money makes the world evolve, not just go around. Having it is holy; having more of it is sacred.

THE GRAND, GALACTIC SCHEME OF LIFE

Each of us fills a vital role as God's proxy on earth. We all have two jobs: our temporal employment and our role as a bit player in the grand, galactic scheme of cosmic evolution that God set into motion when time was new. The two are intimately related, and that is why employment is fundamental to your very nature. Your worldly job may seem insignificant if, for example, you are the custodian for a high school. However, in your role you are fulfilling not only the material need to earn money and the social need to maintain safe and clean schools but the Divine role God ordained for you before you were even born.

I have touched on this before, but now I shall be more precise in my teachings: each of us is God's proxy on the material plane. God is the Spirit and the creative force behind the Universe, but he is a being of pure Spirit and so cannot directly take action on the physical stratum. So he created us, pressing us out of the Divine Mind, in order to act on his behalf. Each of us has been endowed with a role to play in the vast and unknowable drama of creation. Some of us are to raise enlightened children, others to teach; some to advance the cause of science, others to advance the power of medicine. Every single man and woman, no matter how insignificant his or her job may seem, is acting as a small but crucial part in the great cosmic machinery of the evolving world.

When you are idle, you reject your ordained duty and gift from God to stand forth and help to shape the changing fabric of reality. As the Greek poet Hesiod said, "Work is no disgrace: it is idleness which is a disgrace."[2] Employment is payment of the debt we all owe to God for our existence.

Expanding Personal Depth

Nothing can remain static in an active cosmos. Marianne Williamson wrote, "To ask for another relationship, or another job, is not particularly helpful if we're going to show up in the new situation exactly as we showed up in the last one."[3] Change is the rule at all levels of existence, from the lowest bacterium to the pinnacle of humanity. Companies change and grow or they become stagnant. National economies must grow and evolve or they, too, can fall into contraction and ruin. And people must continue to move,

2. Hugh G. Evelyn-White, MA, *Hesiod: the Homeric Hymns and Homerica* (Cambridge, MA: Harvard University Press, 1914), 27.

3. Marianne Williamson, *A Return to Love: Reflections on the Principles of a Course in Miracles* (New York: HarperCollins, 1992), 78.

risk, and dare the unknown in order to fit into the active, fluid nature of the universe.

Work is our source of perennial motion and change. Work is an opportunity not just to earn money but to learn new skills, discover fresh passions, and undergo personal change. From situation to situation, we do not remain the same. We, ourselves, evolve.

CREATING SELF

We are all creators in our own right. We are the direct descendants of God—through his Spirit we were crafted and created, and the unending line of humanity through the ages reflects our Divine heritage. Ecclesiastes 3:22 says, "There is nothing better than that a man should rejoice in his own works, for that is his heritage." We get our purpose and being from God, and as his nature is that of the creator, so is ours. This is the reason so many of us are driven to become entrepreneurs, who are by nature the creators of things that did not previously exist.

This inborn creative impulse must be given free rein, for it is the very heart of our nature. We are all creators—some of us create families, others businesses, others art and music, others churches, others inventions and technologies, and so on. We are continually bringing that which did not previously exist into being with the power of our Minds. Employment is the milieu in which our creative powers can be best used. As we work to find solutions for business problems, build new companies, turn visions into physical realities, and fashion roles and futures for ourselves and those we employ, we act as God in this reality.

Thus the very act of working becomes Divine, because it is through our personal creation that we scale upward and serve the celestial level of creation that has its host and wholeness in God's

Mind. We are the children of the Creator; we were built to create in his name.

At a time in history when employment is scarce, it may seem glib to discuss the finding of a job as the crux of God's purpose. But that is the nature of things, and humankind's wish to take employment from the center of the debate does not change the pivotal nature of having work. A Jewish proverb states, "He that does not bring up his son to some honest calling and employment, brings him up to be a thief." We are meant to seek employment and to be employed at all times. But what does this mean at a time when the unemployment rate is higher than it has been in many years?

In fact, it means nothing in the grand scheme of things. In the short-term, the lack of employment is an educator of people who may have been engaged in employment that was not based on their personal development or spiritual growth but on the need to fill a position wrought by an economic bubble. In other words, nature abhors a vacuum. When a falsely inflated economic situation creates a need for jobs to be filled, some of those jobs will be filled by people who did not earn them but are simply warm bodies. This employment does not serve God's design, which is to have our work mold and elevate us, and because of that it is inevitably doomed. As we have seen, the jobs bred by the economic bubble have vanished like the wind.

Understanding the place of employment in God's system and the Laws means understanding that God's desire is for you to continuously be moving forward—to always be either working or seeking work. Only in this way do you continue to churn up the nutrient of the human ecosystem—money—and feed innovation, creativity, and the fruition of millions of small aspects of God's colossal plan. Work and money breed change and growth. That is their purpose.

THERE IS NO "UNDEREMPLOYMENT" IN GOD'S SYSTEM

According to the Congressional Budget Office, at the lowest point of the last recession, more than twelve million Americans were expected to be underemployed. This means that they were employed in jobs below their level of skill or education. But is it possible to be underemployed in God's eyes? The answer is no. Whatever job you are doing is what you were meant to be doing at this time in your life as part of God's design. Even underemployment can be seen as merely a conduit to something greater, assuming that you do not come to rest but continue to seek something better.

> *This divine law of employment is forever employing and holding us in our right position; that of expressing and living divine qualities no matter what we're doing. The venue may change, but the law is constant.*
>
> —Valerie Minard, "Divine Employment"

Remember, the fact of working is the vital thing; the nature of the work less so. This may seem counterintuitive; you may rage at the idea of working for half of what you made before and struggle to pay your bills, but from a Divine perspective, what matters most is that you are working. Being an active participant in cosmic evolution gives you the forum to create a new opportunity for yourself, to break out of complacency, to strike out on your own after years of working for someone else. Underemployment can have its value, the greatest of which is to ignite the human desire to do more and do better.

So whatever you are doing is holy, even if it is something menial like dishwashing or picking up trash. First of all, these things must be done, and they serve a greater good. Second, the act of being in motion and effecting change even in a small way moves you closer to taking a step upward to a new level of employment. It is far better to be "underemployed" than not employed at all.

Orient Your Mind on Manifestations

Employment in dark times is expertly illustrated in the following story that ran in the *Seattle Examiner*:

> *Fifty years old, at the top of his game and unemployed, Thompson was fed up with the constant reduction in resources and staff. He couldn't do his best work, so he quit. He was certain his experience and truly excellent track record would impress prospective employers as he headed down the job search path with optimism and relief.*
>
> *He ignored the signs that finding new employment would be a challenge: Boeing laid off over 550 people again and even Microsoft finally succumbed to a layoff. Six months later, no new job in hand, Thompson surrendered to disbelief and depression.*
>
> *He had interviewed with people who did not know how to interview. He had interviewed with people with less experience than his, less know-how. He had interviewed with people who were significantly younger. He believed he was overqualified. "These kids running these companies don't have a clue. I intimidate them with my experience and knowledge."*[4]

The problem with this gentleman's approach was not his lack of qualifications but the way in which he used his Mind. He did not

---

4. Rita Ashley, "Over 50 and Still Job Hunting? Part 2," *Seattle Examiner*, August 24, 2009, http://www.examiner.com/executive-careers-in-seattle/over-50-and-still-job-hunting-part-2 (accessed October 2009).

focus on his desire and bring it into being with his I Am intention. Instead, his thoughts were of fear, resentment, and inadequacy, and that is precisely what he reaped from his search. The pivotal factor in the scarcity of work is not the lack of jobs—simply read the classified ads or Craigslist and you will see there are many—but the inability of the employment seeker to focus the power of his or her Divine Mind on the manifestation of the right employment. Fear, anger, hopelessness, and low self-esteem become self-fulfilling emotions as they taint and shatter any incoming stream of Divine manifestation.

When you are seeking work, you cannot dwell on such things. By the Laws of manifestation, the Mind is the currency of the cosmos and calls into being what it gives its attention to (now that is the meaning of the term "to pay attention"!). When you are engaged in a job search, it is vital to envision yourself already ensconced in a position that meets your goals and desires, and to feel surety that such a position will appear. At the same time, understand that such a position may take time; there is no guaranteed time frame for manifestation, and your desires will only come into being when you are ready for them. So if you desire an executive job but only a blue-collar position is available, how do you know that you will not learn some lesson working this "lesser" employment that will make you wiser, stronger, better, and more able to secure the employment of your desire when it appears? All things serve God's purpose, including jobs that appear for the moment to be beneath you. All employment is sacred and should be regarded as such.

RETIREMENT IS NOT NATURAL IN GOD'S SYSTEM

We love the idea of retirement, yet it is a deeply unnatural and unholy thing. On the islands of Okinawa and Sicily, people work all their lives. It is not uncommon to drive the golden hills surrounding Sicily's port of Palermo and find men in their nineties plowing fields, repairing dry-laid rock walls, or herding sheep. They do it happily, and it keeps them young and vital into an age when many Americans have gone to the grave.

Contrast this with American culture, in which millions, according to the latest surveys, plan to retire by age sixty. What will they do after that? Play golf? Watch television? Gamble in casinos? Sit on their porches and rock? Those seem to be the main activities of our "retirement culture," and what have they wrought? We fade into ill health faster than the people of many countries; our cities are filled with idle elders who are seemingly waiting to pass away. Bereft of work or purpose, they do nothing to fulfill their role in God's design, which contributes to their slow erosion toward nothingness.

Retirement is not a natural state for human beings. That does not mean one must work at the same job for sixty years; one should pursue passions and dreams, which are implanted in the Spirit by God. Instead of following a life of working for someone else or in a job that exists simply to pay the bills, each of us should continue to pursue a passion and purpose that is in harmony with the intent of God. This could be public service, mentoring, artistic endeavors, or something similar, but the last thing one should do is just come to a stop. Remember, nothing in the universe can be static without beginning to decay.

WE SHOULD BEGIN WORK
AS EARLY AS POSSIBLE

There is a virtue in employment that has nothing to do with age. The opposite end of the retirement question has to do with beginning employment, and my answer is that it is never too early for children to begin working at home doing chores and discovering how their activity fits into the harmony of God. Aside from the merits of learning discipline, effort, persistence, and the value of money, children as young as seven or eight can also discover the sacred thrill that runs through the Spirit when we are in cadence with the Divine Will and the purpose of the Lord.

Young children can be given jobs like doing the dishes, taking out the trash, or keeping the lawn mowed. In return, they should be paid a wage. This arrangement, a holy compact of sorts with parents or grandparents, activates the child's place in God's system and can begin to bring forth an array of blessings: better performance in school, more savings, greater obedience to parental wishes, and richer moral character. Youth and work should be synonymous rather than mutually exclusive.

For children of poor or lower-middle-class families, work at an early age yields more benefits than I can list here. Studies prove that work and earning income at a young age increases the chances of attending college and avoiding problems like drug use and crime. This is no doubt in part because the young person is working within God's system even before he or she has the maturity to understand the nature of manifestation and the I Am intention. Imagine what can happen when a divinely grounded child finally comes of age! That is how great leaders are born.

TRY TO CREATE JOBS FOR OTHERS

You have certainly heard of the maxim about teaching a man to fish and feeding him for a lifetime. The same dynamic comes into play when you create a job to employ your fellow man who needs work. It is a holy thing to create purpose and activity out of stasis; it is something directly descended from God. This is why entrepreneurs are so respected in the New Thought pantheon: they spark growth and change by allowing others to step into their roles as God's players. When you can create a job and hire your neighbor, you are closer to God than ever.

Does this mean you should employ a person even if you do not have a need for an employee? Yes, if possible. Simply setting a human Mind in motion has effects that cannot be predicted by any human being; when you put the forces of change into action with an act of good and grace, you can produce only positive results. Perhaps the person you hire becomes a source of new business or provides you with a personal service that you need. Perhaps you find a great friend who is with you for life. Creating employment and enabling someone to fulfill part of his Divine destiny is always the right decision!

Employment in our society comes with so much baggage that it is easy to lose sight of its greater meaning and importance. But with this chapter I hope you have gained a vital perspective on the nature of employment and its role in setting your own true employment—as one vital component of the greater Vision of God—in motion.

WHAT WE HAVE LEARNED

- Employment is a fundamental state for anyone who wishes to be in harmony with God.

- You have two jobs: your temporal work to earn money and your role as part of God's cosmic plan.

- Money is the idea of change set free in the world.

- Retirement is unhealthy and unnatural; all beings were meant to be in motion for life.

- Any employment is preferable to idleness.

7

THE LAW OF
ENTANGLEMENT

■ ■ ■ ■ ■

CORE PRINCIPLES

- All is one.

- Separation between individuals is an illusion.

- Every action resounds to the farthest galaxy.

All human beings are interconnected, one with all other elements in creation.

—Henry Reed, English poet

Time after time in my writings I have mounted a direct assault on those who say that science and faith have to be at eternal odds with one another. This chapter is an opportunity to drive home the reality: *science and faith are simply different ways to find the same truth.*

Both are nothing more or less than means to acquiring knowledge of how the Universe operates and what our place within it may be. And as evidenced by organizations like the Institute of Noetic Sciences and the Academy of Spirituality and Paranormal Studies, magazines like *EnlighteNext,* and ongoing conferences and scientific symposia on subjects such as human consciousness and the survival of that consciousness after death, spirituality and science are beginning to collide, to merge.

With new discoveries that quantum mechanics actually functions in the human brain, we are getting closer to decoding the real story behind the Universe: that the cosmos is conscious, that reality is underpinned by a universal Consciousness that we call God and to which we are all forever connected. This truth, which has been talked about by spiritual pioneers and gurus for thousands of years, is only beginning to penetrate the skeptical materialism of modern science, but the progress is steady. A sacred convergence is on the way, when spirituality and science come together into a new discipline that will change our world.

Why do I bring this up? Because the Law of Entanglement (which could also rightly be called the Law of One-Mind) is more closely tied to modern science than any other. The concept of entanglement was first made public in Western, contemporary society by Albert Einstein in 1935. It basically states that any two particles of matter or energy in the universe, once they interact, become permanently entangled. They are bound together forever and will affect one another regardless of distance. This violates all sorts of laws of physics as we know them, so many scientists (Einstein included) disliked entanglement intensely and predicted that it would be falsified by future researchers. But many, many experiments have proven that entanglement is a fact. The book *Entangled Minds* by Dr. Dean Radin is a wonderful way to discover this incredible truth about our universe.

Since all the matter and energy in the cosmos have been around since its creation, every atom has had time to interact with every other atom, which means that everything in the cosmos is entangled—including us.

We are one, after all, you and I. Together we suffer, together exist, and forever will recreate each other.
   —Pierre Teilhard de Chardin, French geologist, philosopher

THE MEANING OF ONENESS

What does this mean for us in our spiritual realm and our discussion of prosperity? Everything. The truth about reality is that nothing is separate. The idea that we are all desperate beings going about our business without affecting anyone else is an illusion. The concept that we can make choices without those choices shaping the lives of everyone on earth is demonstrably false. We are all connected. Every human being in this world is part of one system, each dependent on the other. When someone shows love to her downtrodden sister, it uplifts everyone else in creation in a tiny but real way. Our intentions also affect the stars and galaxies, because they too are entangled with us.

Our intentions affect everything, from large to small. Renowned Japanese scientist Masaru Emoto discovered, after performing a series of experiments, that even water molecules are impacted by our thoughts and feelings. By looking at water under a microscope, Emoto found water crystals would change shape and form depending on the words or feelings projected near the water. Uplifting feelings, such as love, joy, and happiness, created symmetrical, beautiful crystals, while exposure to angry or hateful thoughts and feelings created asymmetrical or distorted crystals—or no crystals at all. If we consider the average adult body is 70 percent water, we come to realize the energy we express to one another affects us on a molecular level. Have you ever felt that pit in your stomach, even when you can't think of anything negative that has been done or said to you or by you? That feeling may be caused by someone else in your life hurting. Emoto said in his book *The Hidden Messages of Water*, "Human consciousness can have an impact on the world around us."

The implications of this for prosperity are enormous. Basically, they prove the truth of the words of Jesus in Matthew 25:40: "Whatever you do to the least of my brothers, that you do unto me." As we deal with the fallout from economic collapse, we can use our awareness of entanglement to notice that no one has escaped harm during this period, not even the rich. Everyone has fallen. But those who have given to others—who have sent vibrations of love, aid, and compassion into the entangled reality by reaching out with a helping or hopeful hand, even as they themselves struggled—have suffered the least.

THE LAW OF ENTANGLEMENT

The things you do that either promote prosperity or prevent it affect not just you but every other person in creation. Choose wisely or you may contribute to economic disaster.

In economics, one of the best illustrations of this law is pioneering economist Adam Smith's "invisible hand," which is also labeled the "law of unintended consequences." Smith said that while each individual seeks only his own gain, he "is led by an invisible hand to promote an end which was no part of his intention. It is not from the benevolence of the butcher, or the baker, that we expect our dinner, but from regard to their own self interest."

Smith's concept was that public good comes about as a side effect of the pursuit of one's own gain, provided that gain is pursued honestly and according to the morals and principles of a fair society (obviously, little or no good came from Enron's pursuit of limitless greed). But in this metaphor do we not also see the invisible hand of God in the Laws that govern the system of the Universe? In this way, you can see that the economics of the material world and the cosmic economics of all reality are quite the same. Words, thoughts and actions have immediate or "local" consequences, but they also radiate outward with "nonlocal" consequences—small outcomes that you may never know of—which affect the lives and futures of many others, and can come around to affect yours as well. As the writer Robert Louis Stevenson said, "Everybody, sooner or later, sits down to a banquet of consequences."[1]

For example, there was a dentist in Southern California who was building a new office for his practice when he decided that he would make some of the space available as exhibit space for local artists. So he remodeled part of the office as a gallery and invited local painters to show their works. The idea was a hit; patients loved the classy addition to the office environment, and artists lined up to exhibit in a low-cost space that had constant traffic flow. End of story, right?

Not quite. Strangely, other artists who had not been part of the dental office project began seeing more opportunities coming their way. Other business owners, entrepreneurs, and philanthropists began developing their own projects that funneled money and visibility to the region's painters, sculptors, and other visual artists. Traffic in local galleries increased dramatically over the next six months. It was as if the dentist had started a snowball rolling with his action, and the goodwill from that action had "broadcast" outward in all directions, sparking others to take similar action. The results benefited thousands more people than those who came in to have their teeth cleaned.

Clearly, the people who were involved in this phenomenon were entangled and were all affected by the dentist's actions. Some were likely affected more strongly, others more weakly, but the unintended consequences radiated from the center and brought economic benefit to many people. Without a doubt, there were millions of other people who felt a less noticeable effect that we can't possibly know about. This is the essence of oneness, that what any one does affects us all. The lesson from the Law of Entanglement is clear: *our financial and economic choices must be made with care because they impact all.*

---

1. http://www.thinkexist.com/english/Author/x/Author_3988_1.htm (accessed October 2009).

THE IMPLICATIONS OF ENTANGLEMENT

William James, the father of modern psychology, said, "This over-coming of all the usual barriers between the individual and the Absolute is the great mystic achievement. In mystic states we both become one with the Absolute and we become aware of our oneness. This is the everlasting and triumphant mystical tradition, hardly altered by differences of clime or creed."[2] James foreshadowed the oneness that is evident in our world but that we have yet to fully grasp, and correctly predicted that it will be transformative. But what does the reality of entanglement mean for our economic present and future? Let's explore that in this chapter.

1. Ideas are contagious.

Have you noticed that inspired new ideas for businesses or products seem to come to many people at the same time? Author Malcolm Gladwell discussed this concept in a column for the *New Yorker*:

> *This phenomenon of simultaneous discovery—what science histo-rians call "multiples"—turns out to be extremely common. One of the first comprehensive lists of multiples was put together by William Ogburn and Dorothy Thomas, in 1922, and they found a hundred and forty-eight major scientific discoveries that fit the multiple pattern. Newton and Leibniz both discovered calculus. Charles Darwin and Alfred Russel Wallace both discovered evolu-tion. Three mathematicians "invented" decimal fractions. Oxygen was discovered by Joseph Priestley, in Wiltshire, in 1774, and by Carl Wilhelm Scheele, in Uppsala, a year earlier. Color photog-raphy was invented at the same time by Charles Cros and by Louis*

---

2. William James, *The Varieties of Human Experience* (Rockville, MD: Arc Manor LLC, 2008), 207.

Ducos du Hauron, in France. Logarithms were invented by John Napier and Henry Briggs in Britain, and by Joost Bürgi in Switzerland ... For Ogburn and Thomas, the sheer number of multiples could mean only one thing: scientific discoveries must, in some sense, be inevitable. They must be in the air, products of the intellectual climate of a specific time and place.[3]

This fact represents One-Mind entanglement beautifully. Because our minds are embedded in the reality of the cosmos that we all share, we all have access to the same universal Mind. We are each part of the fabric of God pressed out, which means that although our ideas may retain the appearance of being our own, locked inside our minds, they are actually shared by all other beings, consciously or subconsciously. Clearly, most people are not enlightened enough to realize this or to leverage that "inspiration superhighway"; if they were, every invention or innovation would have a thousand people battling it out in court over intellectual property ownership. But what this reality means is that even if you develop an idea that can make you rich, you do not have sole ownership. All other Minds in the material world play some role in shaping your idea. So rather than becoming obsessed with legal protection of a new idea, you should work to ensure that your idea benefits all others in some way. A good example of such an enterprise is Craigslist, a free service for those looking for work, homes, cars, or other needs.

2. Selfless action offers tangible benefit.

It is often said that helping others is a blessing on the one who renders aid. For years, some have attributed this to the Hindu concept of

---

3. Malcolm Gladwell, "In the Air: Who Says Big Ideas Are Rare?" *New Yorker*, May 12, 2008, http://www.newyorker.com/reporting/2008/05/12/080512fa_fact_gladwell (accessed October, 2009).

karma, the vague mechanism whereby actions build up a sort of personal "bank account" of good and ill deeds that shapes the person's future. But this is a poorly defined concept; how does karma actually work? Well, entanglement offers us an answer. "What goes around comes around" can be attributed to the reality that each of us is simultaneously connected with all others in the Universe.

When you perform a selfless act of courage or kindness, you are not just aiding the person on the scene at that moment. You are also setting in motion a cascade of compassionate energy that passes through the invisible fabric of the cosmos like an electrical current, bringing hope and healing to each Spirit it comes into contact with. The spread of the effect of good deeds and selfless thoughts can only benefit you in the long run, as you too are entangled with the rest of humankind—and with God as well. So helping someone in need find shelter or quit using drugs will inevitably return to you in tangible form in some unforeseeable future time as a new job, a financial windfall, the healing of an illness, the appearance of someone beneficial in your life, or something else entirely.

This is why churches that aggressively engage in works of public good thrive financially and in terms of the health of their congregations. Not only are they improving the fertility of the soil in which they grow their futures (an idea I discuss in the next chapter) but they create a storm of good, giving energy that eventually comes back to them in more than one form as money, opportunity, new people, or new knowledge.

3. You will create your own loaves and fishes.
In Matthew 14:13–21, Mark 6:34–44, Luke 9:10–17, and John 6:1–13, the Bible talks about the miracle of the loaves and fishes, in which Jesus multiplies scant food to feed a throng that has come to

hear him teach. This is a prime example of the power of the Divine Mind to manifest thought, when there is perfect faith in the reality of that thought, but it is also entanglement in action.

One of the factors that made Jesus's miracle possible was the presence of all the Minds at the gathering. You see, because each person partakes of the Mind of God and possesses the Divine ability to manifest, the entangled Minds and Spirits of others who are the focus of a Divinely inspired action act as magnifiers of the I Am intention. So the people he was trying to feed actually helped Jesus complete his miracle—they were cocreators of it! This dynamic actually plays out in our entangled economy. As you put forth business ideas, seek opportunities, or try to create profitable relationships, keep in mind that you are not working alone. The Minds in your sphere of influence will partake of your thoughts and energy and magnify their power. This magnification is greater when some of the people around you are enlightened and aware of Divine Mind, but this ability is inherent in humanity, so even if they are unaware, they will increase your ability to know and manifest great things.

The power of the collective Mind is beautifully demonstrated in the Global Consciousness Project, an ongoing experiment run by scientists around the world. Convinced that all Minds are entangled, the creators of the GCP hypothesized that when important, emotional events are experienced simultaneously by billions of people, the focused collective Mind increases the order of the Universe. This effect can be measured by observing how the increased focus reduces randomness. The scientists set up random-number generators around the world and began monitoring their output of numbers, which at any given time should be completely chaotic. But after events like the death of Princess Diana and 9/11, they found that randomness was reduced. Minds perceiving in sync actually bring order to the cosmos! This is the potential of entanglement.

4. No one is alone.

The monk Thomas Merton said, "Love is our true destiny. We do not find the meaning of life by ourselves alone—we find it with another."[4] The loneliness of economic troubles can be terrifying. When we lose a job, lose a home, lose health insurance ... the humiliation and fear can make us withdraw into a shell, blaming God and envying others who are not in our plight. It becomes very easy to go the route of John, who fled human contact to live in a cave and eventually write the book of Revelation, which reveals a deeply disturbed mind. Our sanity demands human contact, and nowhere are we more alone than when our minds shy away from others even as our bodies walk in the sun.

Then it is uplifting and hopeful to remember that oneness is the true essence of humankind. God created us not only to be eternally linked to him, but to each other. Do not let your senses deceive you: no one is alone. Even when you are in the depths of your despair, you are not abandoned by your fellow travelers. Everyone else in the corporeal world is a part of you, and you share a part of your being with all who reside in this reality. God is always with us, but even more so in the connection and interconnection—Mind, Body, and Spirit—that exists among his children and can never be broken.

Entanglement's ability to unify science and the spiritual is demonstrated again with the Templeton Prize, given to scientific work that affirms "life's spiritual dimension." Great physicists like Frenchman Bernard d'Espagnat continue to labor, looking for proof that Mind and Consciousness are real, not illusory, entities that have the power of cause and effect. That we in the spiritual world already know this to be true does not lessen the impact.

---

4. Thomas Merton, Naomi Burton, and Patrick Hart, *Love and Living* (New York: HoughtonMifflin Harcourt, 2002), 27.

You Cannot Disentangle Yourself from the Cosmos

Physicists say that because all the atoms and molecules that make up our bodies and brains were formed billions of years ago when God set in motion the events that led to the Big Bang, every bit of matter and energy in the cosmos has been in contact with every other bit. Therefore, everything, from stars to the smallest quark, is forever entangled and linked regardless of distance. And no, there is nothing you can do about it.

This can be unnerving for some. Einstein famously called entanglement "spooky action at a distance," in part because it violated his special law of relativity, but also because the idea of infinite connections unaffected by distance spooked him with its implications. Could we all partake of each other's thoughts? Would we still be individuals? Those are all questions that come to mind.

There are no actions any of us can take to disentangle from the fabric of the cosmos. Even God cannot become unentangled from the rest of us; having set down the Laws of reality, he must obey them. But God would not want to separate from humanity, for we are him in this world, and we are doing his work. Being entangled with humankind allows God to express his will to us when we pray, meditate, or sit in quiet contemplation—when we can fully grasp the wholeness of the oneness we share.

So entanglement is a good and great thing, something to be celebrated. Revel in it if you choose, but do not fear it. It is the natural order of things, and makes possible the many wonders we call "paranormal," such as the laying on of healing hands and the seeing of things happening far away. The wonders of consciousness are possible because we all share in a single experience. We are one family. We are One-Mind.

A miracle is nothing more or less than this. Anyone who has come into a knowledge of his true identity, of his oneness with the all-pervading wisdom and power, this makes it possible for laws higher than the ordinary mind knows of to be revealed to him.

—Ralph Waldo Trine, *In Tune with the Infinite*

EVEN BUSINESSES ARE ENTANGLED

Each business is a human enterprise, so of course all businesses are entangled with all else in existence. The implications of this are profound for anyone who owns a company or runs a small business. Essentially, when you are forced to lay off people or even shut down your business because of tough economic times, are you sending out a wave of misfortune into the entangled fabric of humanity and helping to nudge other business toward ruin?

Yes and no. Yes, any action that we take has effects that resonate from us in three dimensions like the ripples from a stone thrown in a pond, and it affects future generations. Onondagan Oren Lyons, quoted in Steve Wall and Harvey Arden's *Wisdomkeepers*, said, "With every decision we make, we always keep in mind the Seventh Generation to come.... When we walk upon Mother Earth we always plant our feet carefully because we know the faces of our future generations are looking up at us from beneath the ground." Each of us affects another, whether the action is large or small. So it is inevitable that when a business owner is forced by circumstances to close or let people go, the impact of that act vibrates through the spiritual fabric of things. The results? Well, other entrepreneurs who are on the fence about laying off workers may decide to do so. Companies that are hanging on by their fingernails may get that last tiny piece of bad news that pushes them over the edge. Our actions can resonate into the ether and cause more damage, sadly.

However, it is vital to keep in mind that it is not only the nature of our actions in running a business that matters but the spirit in which we take them. Ours is a mental universe where intention is the ultimate power source. So if you operate a restaurant and are forced because of declining business to let 20 percent of your staff go, but do it with compassion and offers to help them find other jobs, your kindness also flies into the cosmos and affects others. Thus, even a choice that appears negative and hurtful on its surface can ultimately produce a positive overall effect on the world if it is just and fair and taken in a spirit of love and goodwill. As comedian Margaret Cho said, "Sometimes when we are generous in small, barely detectable ways it can change someone else's life forever."[5]

Secrets in an Entangled Universe

Do the people in your life know your most private thoughts? Very likely, they do not. Though many parapsychologists and consciousness researchers believe that entanglement is what makes telepathy possible, they also agree that we are not all reading each other's deepest thoughts all the time. Your privacy in your own head is safe.

The effect of entanglement on all but the tiniest percentage of people who are fully enlightened and have the full use of the Divine powers of Mind is small but potent. Your thoughts and actions do not control the Minds of others, but instead influence the direction and tenor of other people's thoughts, emotions, and spiritual orientation. So a positive frame of mind not only lifts your spirits but also becomes contagious, lending a slight nudge toward inspiration and hope to all those around you, even those with whom you have no direct contact.

---

5. Jack Canfield, Mark Victor Hansen, Patty Hansen, and Irene Dunlap, *Chicken Soup for the Kids Soul 2* (Deerfield Beach, FL: HEI, 2006), 91.

It is this same dynamic that allows healing thoughts to foster healing, new ideas to bring about creative bursts from all corners, and thoughts of hatred and violence to breed more of their evil. Our thoughts are like cartoon images of angels and devils, sitting on the shoulders of others and whispering in their ears.

The only exception to this truth is that you cannot hide from God. You, and all of us, are part and parcel of the fabric of the Consciousness of God, who is the Great Underlying Consciousness, the Universal Mind. Being pure Spirit and pure Mind, God dwells at a level of awareness where all thought is instantly transparent. This is why you can neither hide from yourself nor from God. It is also why the undisciplined Mind may cause damage to others but hurts itself most of all.

ENTANGLEMENT CAN ATTRACT GOOD FORTUNE

The principle of entanglement suggests many economic applications, none greater than the ability to attract like-minded people and influence their thinking. In a way, leveraging this Law is the ultimate tool of an effective leader, because a person with the mental discipline to orient his or her Mind on positive outcomes, hope, creativity, and energy subtly but effectively shapes the Minds of others. Imagine the power in radiating a "can't fail" mind-set when you are trying to start a business. It's I Am manifestation applied to our world, emotions, and motivation.

In the same way, entanglement can be used to attract you to people who think as you think. The more enlightened and spiritually aware you become, the more you attract individuals who share those qualities. This means that our mind-sets really are self-fulfilling prophecies that determine our fortunes. However, you will attract and influence others only to the degree that your intentions fit the intentions of God: creating, healing, and manifesting abundance. If you seek to manipulate, cheat, or intimidate others into doing as you wish, your underlying emotions and thoughts show through, and you will influence them in ways that do not benefit you—and could even sabotage you. Mental discipline is important, but truth in intent and strong morality are just as critical.

What We Have Learned

- We are all one in the fabric of the cosmos.

- Everything in the universe influences everything else.

- Mental states can influence the minds and actions of others.

- Entanglement is permanent.

- It can attract great fortune if used with justice and morality.

8

THE LAW OF FERTILITY

■ ■ ■ ■ ■

CORE PRINCIPLES

- Treat the environment of "beingness" around you as the soil for your growth.

- Every action you take tills that soil to serve your future prosperity.

- You must plant what is best suited for your ground and then nurture it.

The human mind cannot create anything. It produces nothing until after having been fertilized by experience and meditation; its acquisitions are the gems of its production.

—Georges-Louis Leclerc Buffon, French naturalist

In Matthew 17:20, Jesus says, "Because of your unbelief; for verily I say unto you, If ye have faith of a grain of mustard seed, ye shall say unto this mountain, Remove hence to yonder place; and it shall remove; and nothing shall be impossible unto you." Both ideas dovetail into a single concept: that of sowing and fertility. It is impossible to escape the metaphor of the farm in an age of economic anxiety. We have come to live at a time when, out of necessity, we are being forced back to our roots: smaller businesses, local economies, sustainability, and simplicity. And while these ideas may prove to be fads to a degree, at some level they will sustain themselves and carry on in parallel to the resurgence of our larger, global economy.

The point is this, revealed to us both by biblical wisdom and by the wisdom of the marketplace: no one can rely on a market or economy-by-proxy to sow the seeds of his or her own prosperity. When our enterprises become so large and our systems so complex that we are each divorced from the manifestation of our own fortunes, we become like the farmer whose farm has grown from a family forty acres to a huge industrial operation: we lose knowledge and control. And we cannot lose control because our fates are our own responsibility. So we come to the Law of Fertility.

The Bible talks about seedtime and harvest, and that each comes in its own season. We cannot control the seasons of the earth. In fact, none of us has any idea when the seasons of our lives come to pass; they do not come in orderly progression: spring, summer, autumn, winter. No ... you can experience a spring in your life and then, through poor planning and arrogance, jump right to a winter of discontent. Human seasons are capricious. But you can prepare for any season by readying the soil of yourself and your environment to produce the highest prosperity benefit—as Samuel Smiles observed, "Sow a thought, and you reap an act; Sow an act, and you reap a habit; Sow a habit, and you reap a character; Sow a character, and you reap a destiny."[1]

You cannot hold on to anything good. You must be continually giving—and getting. You cannot hold on to your seed. You must sow it—and reap anew. You cannot hold on to riches. You must use them and get other riches in return.

—Robert Collier, *Riches Within Your Reach*

ON "BEINGNESS"

Action is the seed that must be sown, and economic prosperity is the eventual crop you reap. But prior to sowing, what does the wise farmer do? He prepares the soil; he adds compost, fertilizer, nitrogen, and manure, and lets the land rest and lie fallow for a season to become fertile. He does all these things to ensure that the ground is fertile for what he intends to plant. This is the same process you must undergo as you work to retake control of your own life's crop and make it sustainable in good times and hard.

1. Ronald D. Anron, *God's Seven Ways to Ease Suffering* (Longwood, FL: Xulon Press, 2007), 219.

Consider that what the farmer adds to his soil are called *amendments*. This is the same term used to describe additions to the US Constitution; for example, the added passage that outlawed slavery was the Thirteenth Amendment. So an amendment is that which promotes change. It does not bring about the change on its own, but it sets the stage for it, making the ground ready for the planting of new ideas and a new future. With the system of God as your constitution, you must make the soil fertile and add your own amendments, so change can come into your economic life. When times are hard and you cannot see your way to immediate hope, fertilize the soil. Eventually, new growth will appear, but only if your ground is prepared.

THE LAW OF FERTILITY

When your immediate economic circumstances are dire, you must work to make the soil of your "beingness" fertile for new prosperity to take root.

What is *beingness*? *Beingness* is the term used by the great Eckhart Tolle that describes the essence of the existence of a person or thing—the Spirit behind the material. But in the context of our conversation on prosperity, *beingness* has a wider connotation: the entire sphere of what makes you *you*. Your beingness is the sum of your relationships, ideas, habits, Mind, health, practices, knowledge, biases, and connection with God. All of it. Those are the seeds of your prosperity in the physical world. When harvest time comes, what you reap will be a direct consequence of how fertile your beingness was even while times were hard.

This, in fact, is the purpose of the cycles and seasons of life: to allow us the space and time to tend to the garden of our beingness. Think on this—does a person fortify a house when it is not falling down? Does someone rewrite a great work of fiction or poetry? No. We reexamine and remake ourselves only in times of struggle and crisis. A man who has been obese all his life may only "get religion" about exercise and diet after he has a heart attack. Why? Because we live in the moment, and complacency deceives us into thinking that we can remain static and healthy. But as we saw with the Law of Employment, God did not design a static universe. Everything is designed to move, change, and evolve. We are designed for the same. So when you lose your job, have no money, or are faced with economic uncertainty, these are times to rejoice. These are the seasons when we grow and evolve into new forms, something we will never do while we are secure and self-satisfied.

PREPARING THE SOIL

How do you tend your beingness and prepare it for future growth? First, you must understand one of the most basic, essential truths of the cosmos: *you are money.*

Money is the energy of God in the world. You are an agent of God charged with effecting transformative change in the physical world; you are created to be the custodian of money. You are meant to have its limitless supply, to have it flow freely through your fingers, and to project it outward to create positive change for others. Wealth is native to your being. You were born to prosperity.

Once you understand this, you will begin to access money on all levels: emotional, psychological, and physical. Money is an exchange of energy. That is why when you transform your consciousness, true wealth must be given to you. So, in preparing the soil of your being-ness, you must change yourself. Your beingness extends out from you like an aura in all directions, but it begins with your Mind, your Spirit, your ideas, and your love for yourself and others. To create fertile soil for wealth to come, you must begin by working to purify and discipline your:

- Mind
- Thoughts
- Habits
- Spiritual practices
- Gratitude and love for others

You are the channel through which money flows, so it only follows that to receive wealth you must first make yourself fertile ground for its growth. Orienting your Mind on your I Am intention and mentally becoming that which you desire is that first step. Having the discipline to reject all negative thinking and continuously focus your Divine Mind on that invisible reality is the second step. You must also find your generosity, honor, and commitment to others. Money wants to be used and spent on great works. As Florence Scovill Shinn wisely wrote:

Money is God in manifestation, as freedom from want and limitation, but it must be always kept in circulation and put to right uses. Hoarding and saving react with grim vengeance. This does not mean that man should not have houses and lots, stocks and bonds, for the barns of the righteous man shall be full; it means man should not hoard even the principal, if an occasion arises, when money is necessary. In letting it go out

fearlessly and cheerfully, he opens the way for more to come in,
for God is man's unfailing and inexhaustible supply.[2]

If you don't have a great deal of money to spend and share with others, then spend yourself. Share your time, your support, your ideas, or your sweat. Kathy LeMay advised in her book *The Generosity Plan* that we use the "time, talent, and treasure" model of philanthropy which, LeMay wrote, work together in service to the greater good. Money alone does not make a difference—it needs our time and our talents to work. How can your talent, or skills and training, benefit others? How can you spend your time assisting those in need? If you wish to know abundance, you must first create abundance—and this is not a catch-22. There are many ways to be wealthy and know abundance. Preparing your beingness to be fertile for true wealth demands that you give everything you have today as a down payment for tomorrow.

THE CROP

When you have begun preparing the soil of yourself, then you must move on to other aspects of your beingness that are purely external:

- Your relationships
- Your home
- Your possessions
- Your community

---

2. Florence Scovel Shinn, *The Game of Life and How to Play It* (Los Angeles: Forgotten Books, 2008), 53.

The astonishing thing to understand about money is that, because money is a manifestation of the power of God to effect change, the following must be true: *money is a conscious force.*

The cosmic consciousness that wraps around money wants to know that its custodians will be spiritually and mentally ready to use money in the best way possible—to aid others, to help bring about enlightened change, and to inspire more people to discover their own Divinity. In essence, you must evolve in all ways to be an ideal, fertile ground for the seeds of wealth to be planted and grow. That means not only transforming your Mind and Spirit but also showing that you can become the wealth that you seek. Severing relationships with individuals who drain your energy or funnel it into negative or self-destructive pursuits should be at the top of the priority list. Relationships tell the truth about who we are no matter how we might try to conceal that truth from ourselves. Your relationships must point to your spiritual evolution if you are to manifest abundance.

Beyond that, work on the physical trappings of your life to cloak yourself in the reality of wealth. Redesign your living space to be richer, more inviting, and more indicative of wealth. Exhibit an outward air of confidence in your own destiny as a person of true wealth. Work with your community to bring about positive change. Be a leader. Be creative. Be a creator in your flesh! That is the type of soil in which wealth wishes to embed deeply and grow.

The concept of fertility is all about putting your faith in the future when your present is one of want and lack of opportunity— or at least, not the kind of opportunity you crave. It is about looking beyond current circumstances to see what your life can be and preparing the way for abundance to arrive in your experience. In this way, it is very much an act of seeing the future—of precognition. Carried out to its logical conclusion, following the Law of

Fertility is a godlike course of living in your own future before it comes to pass. That is the mark of true spiritual maturity and something truly crucial to strive for.

How You Will Know Your Soil Is Fertile

Wealth can come in many forms: finances, emotions, community pride, health, and so on. When you are first tilling and amending the soil of your soul (remember the connection between the two words this way: replace the i of *soil* with a u, or *you*, to get *soul*), you may not see vast changes in your experience. But over time, as you continue to make your beingness more fertile, you will begin to perceive new wealth entering your orbit:

- New relationships with movers and shakers will come your way.
- A new job will be offered to you.
- Investors will appear to become part of your business idea.
- Debts will be cancelled.
- A house that was previously beyond your means will drop in price to be within your means.

This is the harbinger of the fact that you are doing well in your fertility choices: greater wealth descends on your life in a consistent rainfall of good fortune. When you see someone living in poverty, it's a sure sign that he or she has let his or her personal soil become fouled with pessimism, defeatism, lack of faith, and lack of hope. The hard work of faith—the optimism of tomorrow in the face of the pessimism of today—is too much for some. They believe in fairy godmother God who grants wishes out of nowhere. They know nothing of the truth that they are God in this world and they need not wait for anyone to grant them anything.

Wealthy entrepreneurs have invested in the belief that their ideas are sound, that they have the power to make them reality, and that they can and will come to pass. This is why determination is often cited as the most important attribute of the successful entrepreneur. Refusing to surrender your faith in your power to manifest makes manifestation possible. When you steadily till your soil with discipline, wealth begins to grow. This is a sign that you are on the right path.

WEALTH, LIKE FERTILITY, COMES IN SEASONS

I have said before that there is a difference between knowing God and knowing his Kingdom. Money is creative power, and so it is equal to God. It is the only force to have that status. Money is potential energy waiting to be used. When you buy something, you are buying it with the energy of your Mind. That money in your pocket is not real money; it is the result of money. The real money of the cosmos is the energy of your Divine Mind. The Kingdom of God is the economic system that enables you to manifest this creative force with your Mind, if applied in the right ways.

Understanding the nature of wealth also means understanding that it flows and ebbs, as do all things in nature. Yes, in nature. Money is a force for evolution, no different in its effect than flowing water or blasting wind, except that money is conscious and responds to Consciousness. In nature, all things come in seasons, and that is also true of wealth. You must know your seedtime from your harvest time. By knowing this, you will prepare when preparation is called for and not try to harvest when you should be planting, nor plant when you should be reaping the results of your faith and discipline. God-ordained wealth does not come to you consistently. You must take action according to the proper season and have the patience to let people and actions come to their proper conclusions.

You will see the seasons when you become a keener observer of the Divine nature of the world—when you train yourself to perceive the subtle signs that others overlook. You will note when spring comes, because it is the time when opportunities present themselves for your approval or rejection: planting time. Summer shows itself as the period when you must protect your crop of wealth by spreading it around to others and creating abundance for your community. Pay close attention to summer, because extending the power of your wealth energy into the lives of others is vital in order to continue harvesting additional wealth.

Autumn is harvest time, which manifests as incoming wealth: the closing on a long-desired home, a huge sale, or a big investment contract being signed. It is the time to celebrate with your own harvest festival. And winter is the time to become quiet and contemplative, to learn from what has gone before, and to sow your seeds for the coming cycle. It is the greatest time of learning and of reaching out to create new relationships.

FERTILITY CAN BE LOST JUST AS IT IS GAINED

Sometimes, crops fail. Sometimes, you have a bumper crop one season and nothing the next. You can lose fertility; nothing is guaranteed. What does it take to strip your beingness of the wealth energy that brings about change? Well, these are some examples of fertility-draining choices:

- You hoard your wealth instead of projecting it outward into the community where it can elevate the Spirits of others and carry them toward their own enlightenment. Wealth wants to walk the streets, get with the people, and provoke transformation in the lives of all who come into contact with it. If you grasp it too roughly so it cannot bring blessings to others, it will run through your fingers.

- You become so enamored with your wealth that your mental discipline of manifestation fades. You begin to believe that you are the source of the abundance and praise yourself for it. Instead, you must remember that God's system is the source, and you are only the conduit of that wealth; a vital role, to be sure, but not the same as being the source. Giving in to ego can cost you all you gave gained.

- You fall into the corruption of false relationships. People of all stripes will be drawn to your abundance. If your Mind is true and focused on good and honor, most of those are people of moral virtue who can multiply your wealth. However, some are grasping, desperate, or manipulative. You must have the presence of mind to cast those people from your circle without mercy, for they will poison your spiritual enterprise if you allow them to. Those whose focus is on drugs, sex, fraud, or illegality should be treated as pestilence and shunned. People of good character are your greatest business.

- You forget the seasons. Attempting to harvest in winter, say, or to plant in summer, reaps you nothing but dust and frustration. You must always be aware of the signs that a new season is coming and know the proper actions. For example, if business slows and quiets, it is a sign that winter is coming. Trying to plant a new business opportunity during such a time will waste your wealth.

ORGANIC WEALTH

Organic agriculture is extremely popular, and its metaphor extends beautifully into our world of the spiritual and the manifestation of wealth. As you may know, organic food is that which has been produced without the introduction of anything manufactured by humans: pesticides, herbicides, hormones, or antibiotics. It is considered the healthiest way to grow and eat, in part because it helps preserve the natural balance of the soil and the ecosystem.

In the spiritual ecosystem of abundance and its harvest, the idea of organic refers to the manifestation of wealth in which the receiver relies on nothing but the hand of God and his system to provide all sustenance and support. It is wealth that comes about in an environment completely free of manmade contingency plans that the individual has in place just in case the system does not provide the abundance it is supposed to. In other words, if you declare your I Am and rely on God's economic machine to bring you an entrepreneurial opportunity, yet while you wait for that to manifest you keep your old job just in case things don't work out, you are poisoning your harvest. God's system works at its pinnacle when we depend entirely on it and nothing else as our means of bread and life.

Here is an example: A professional athlete in a sport that does not pay great amounts of money was working on the book that would tell the story of her life. As anyone (myself included) who has published a book can tell you, it is hardly a guarantee of riches. While she worked and waited for fortune to strike and trained for her events, the athlete went more and more into debt until she had virtually nothing. But she refused loans and other help. She was also a person of faith and she relied on God's system to be her means of support. She knew if she focused on her manifestation and her vision, God would bring fortune into her orbit. As the months went by, she got new sponsors, a national award, and wide publicity, and became a sought-after speaker. God answered her organic desire with a bountiful harvest of abundance.

You may not be in a position to leave your job and rely only on God's largesse as your safety net. That is as it may be; we must live in the world and in Spirit as best we can. But if you want to manifest the greatest good and the purest blessing, try to cast aside any forms of hedging or contingency plans and rely on Spirit as much as you can.

The Law of Fertility is straightforward, but its application can be confounding. To master it, you must become adept at reading the signs of the changing seasons in the same way that a farmer is able to read the weather, rainfall, and insect population. You must hone and refine your ability to perceive the subtleties of God's Mind and witness the clockwork of manifestation as it operates. This takes time and dedication, but when you can learn to prepare your being-ness for abundance in the proper way, you will find that bounties of good fortune can be yours.

WHAT WE HAVE LEARNED

- Difficult times can be ideal times to prepare your beingness for the coming harvest of abundance.

- You are the soil in which blessings are planted.

- Your crop is meant to be shared with others; hoarding will ruin your future harvest.

- There are seasons for planting, weeding, and preparing.

- The richest blessings come when you rely only on Spirit for support and do not hedge your bets.

9

The Law of Hidden Patterns

Core Principles

- The courses of fortune are inherently unpredictable.

- Forecasting your own future is a fool's game.

- You have two courses of action to shape your ends: preparation and response.

We sleep, but the loom of life never stops, and the pattern which was weaving when the sun went down is weaving when it comes up in the morning.

—Henry Ward Beecher, *US congregational minister*

A while back, some new research came out that tied the geomagnetic field to the ups and downs of the stock market. Researchers showed that when the geomagnetic field that surrounds the Earth is at its strongest, people's emotions are more volatile, and therefore there is more panic in the global economy's markets. When the field is quiet, people are calmer and make more rational decisions.

Hey, it's as good a metric as any for predicting the movement of something that's inherently unpredictable. The fact is, people have been trying for centuries to predict when and how the markets are going to rise and fall. Some have been charlatans, most have been well-intentioned but misguided, and all of them have been unsuccessful. If anyone had been able to reliably predict share prices, he or she would have been a billionaire many times over. But no one has been able to do it. There is a factor of randomness and unpredictability built into the DNA of the market, because it is a human construct with billions of moving parts: us.

Take this principle and apply it to the sphere of cosmic manifestation and human prosperity, and you arrive at the situation we are in as enlightened beings. We want to know what is to come, to believe that we have control over our futures. Many philosophers have claimed for years that the primary reason humans need to believe in a God or Supreme Being is because it is a way to deal with the fear of death. But I disagree. I think that the greater fear is actually the fear of chaos: the fear that there is no plan for life—that terrible things happen for no reason and that everything is random. We crave predictability.

The Law of Hidden Patterns speaks directly to this fear and offers us comfort. It imposes a kind of quiet order on what seems to be chaos and meaninglessness. Of course, as enlightened believers, we already know that God Consciousness is real and that we are destined to rise to a higher plane of existence when our time on this physical earth is over. That fear is put to rest. But the other great terror—chaos and randomness—can seem overwhelming at times, even to someone of the highest spiritual Mind. That is understandable; our Minds are small in comparison with the Mind of God. We have only the tiniest fraction of the perception that he has of all places, all people, and all times, past and future. In dwelling outside of time and beyond the limitations of physical dimension, God can see all things as they have developed, are developing, and will develop. We must rely on faith.

LIFE IS LIKE THE STOCK MARKET

If you invest in the stock market, you know that it is a system built on one step forward, one step back. Historical research reveals that most of the big gains in the markets are made during only about ten big days per year; the rest of the time, stock prices are advancing as people buy, and then retreating as they sell to take their profits.[1] It

---

1. Mike Rowan, "You Can Lose 1/2 of Your Investment Returns by Missing the 10 Best Days? September 15, 2009, http://shine.yahoo.com/channel/life/you-can-lose-1-2-of-your-investments-by-missing-the-10-best-days-512833 (accessed October 2009).

can be maddening to try to "time the market." If you do, you virtually guarantee that you will lose out on big gains and damage your prospects for long-term wealth.

> *Predictions of the future are never anything but projections of present automatic processes and procedures, that is, of occurrences that are likely to come to pass if men do not act and if nothing unexpected happens; every action, for better or worse, and every accident necessarily destroys the whole pattern in whose frame the prediction moves and where it finds its evidence.*
>
> —**Hannah Arendt**, *Crises of the Republic*

However, there exists an underlying pattern in this chaotic financial ecosystem—a repeating, predictable occurrence. It is this: eventually, if you wait long enough, there will be a sudden, dramatic shift in the market's direction, a bounce. If you are in the market when this bounce comes, you can regain six months' losses in a single week, sometimes in a single day. No one can predict when a bounce will come (or a crash, for that matter), but the study of the past ensures that it will come. No market goes down forever.

Life and the stock market have much in common. Both are complex organic systems built on a delicate balance between the drive of our emotions and the planning and foresight of our reason. And like the stock market, the concept of the bounce exists in life. It is the underlying pattern in the chaos: given enough time, our fortunes will take an abrupt and dramatic shift for the better. This is inevitable, but it is also incumbent upon us to be prepared for that shift and to leverage it when it happens. The other key factor in this equation is this: *there is no knowing when the bounce in life will occur.*

This is the hidden pattern in the progress of our futures, the seemingly random placement of a great shift in our prosperity that will always come, making it not so random after all. But just as the investor who has not put money into the market will not be able to take advantage of the sharp market jumps that come out of nowhere, neither can your enlightened Divine Mind take advantage of your own bounce unless you are prepared for it when it arrives. This leads to the Law of Hidden Patterns:

THE LAW OF HIDDEN PATTERNS

Within the seeming chaos of life is a dynamic like the stock market: the hidden certainty of a sudden jump in good fortune that we must be prepared to leverage when it comes.

There are two ways this principle can show up. Either in the form of sudden life, or sudden death.

SUDDEN LIFE

A fine example of this principle in action came in the person of Susan Boyle, whom you may have seen on YouTube in the spring of 2009, along with a few million others. Susan was a Scottish woman in her fifties who had never dated and lived alone with her cats. But she was an accomplished singer who had never given up on her dream of one day being a professional singer. As a result, she continued to work on her vocal abilities despite the incredible odds against her dream ever coming true.

Then, fatefully, she appeared on the British television program *Britain's Got Talent*—the precursor to *American Idol*. Facing an audience that had prejudged her for her rather dowdy appearance, she wowed the audience and judges with an incredible song. Overnight, she became an international celebrity. Though in the end she finished second on the show, she sparked the beginnings of a singing career and has already released her first album.

That is an example of the fundamental idea that allows us to fully use the Law of Hidden Patterns: doing the right things consistently over time without needing encouragement that they will pay off. Susan Boyle could not have known that her constant work on her singing would ever lead to international fame and a career, but that did not matter; she kept working regardless. When the bounce in her fortunes came, she was psychologically and spiritually prepared to take full advantage. Her dedication and discipline paid huge dividends. She could not possibly have known when the shift in her fortunes would arrive, but when it did, she was prepared for it due to her unflagging devotion. As Sir Francis Bacon said, "The way of fortune is like the Milky Way in the sky; which is a number of smaller stars, not seen asunder, but giving light together; so it is a number of little and scarce discerned virtues, or rather faculties and customs, that make men fortunate."[2]

SUDDEN DEATH

The other extreme can be seen in the consequences of an unusual series of incidents that occurred during the California gold rush of the nineteenth century. Daniel Hill, a gold prospector in Northern California, found not one but two enormous gold nuggets lying out in the open. The sale of the nuggets brought him a total of $19,000—equivalent to $345,503 in today's dollars. This sum should

---

2. Francis Bacon, *The Works of Lord Bacon* (London: Henry G. Bohn, 1854), 294.

have kept Hill in luxury for years, but he burned through the money (not just once but twice) in less than a week, spending it primarily on alcohol and prostitutes.

A French prospector during the same time found a huge nugget worth $5,000 ($143,726 in today's dollars), and the sudden wealth made him act so erratically and violently that the next day he was sent to an asylum for the mentally incompetent. What does all this say? It says that sudden turns of fortune—especially in the areas related to career, wealth, and prosperity—can become blessings or curses depending on what we have done to prepare our Mind, Spirit, and character to respond to the bounce when it comes. Preparation and response are wealth creators in God's system. They can be the difference between life and death when fortunes shift without warning.

PREPARE AND RESPOND

So what are you to do to avoid the fate of the gold prospectors? If you cannot know when the sudden shift in your personal stock market is going to come, how can you prepare for it? You cannot prepare for specific events because you simply lack the cosmic consciousness to know what is going to happen. Some few individuals, such as prophets and psychics, who possess the gift of precognition (something that is beginning to be proved in controlled experiments, one of the most exciting developments in connecting spirituality and science) may be able to glimpse the future and even predict events, but no one can offer specifics: which stock to buy, where to move, what college degree to get so you're ready for the incredible job offer that will come in three years.

Only God possesses that knowledge, and that is wise. If we knew what was going to occur in our lives before it happened, we could easily become either paralyzed with fear or complacent in believing that our future good fortune is assured. However, as the Law of Hidden Patterns tells us, good fortune is not simply a matter of the timeline of a human life intersecting with the inevitable progress of a beneficial event. The bounce that brings you wealth, security, and abundance comes in two parts:

1. Your life's through line intersects with the source of the good fortune: you get a marvelous job offer, inherit a fortune, or sell a book for a million dollars.

2. You react appropriately to the bounce based on your character and enlightenment and turn it to its maximum advantage.

Both halves of the equation must be in place for you to realize the greatest outcome and the richest prosperity from God's system. If your sudden shift in fortunes occurs but your response is based on greed, ego, or fear, you will waste it. A case in point is the story of the prodigal son, whose father gifted him with great wealth that the son went forth and squandered on frivolities. The other son, who remained at home and was responsible, showed the character to make the most of his own good fortune.

So what are we to do in order to be prepared to respond wisely and productively to the bounce in our fortunes when it comes, as it surely will? Since we cannot take specific steps, we must instead refine our Spirits, hone our Minds, and burnish our personal characters and values. In this way, when the unknowable increase in our fortunes does come, we will be ready to take full advantage of it, by having built a foundation of mental and personal qualities that serves us in any situation. There is no purpose in the course of our cosmic evolution that is not be served by greater discipline, deeper care for other individuals, a stronger creative mind, or greater knowledge of finance.

To fully leverage the Law of Hidden Patterns, you need to focus on:

- Cleansing your life of destructive relationships with people whose only interest is exploitation or personal pleasure at the expense of others
- Refining your character by putting more time into caring about others, helping those less fortunate, developing your personal sense of virtue and values, and delaying gratification in favor of long-term growth
- Practicing discipline and hard work in developing the skills you feel will be most useful in realizing your prosperity vision, from financial management and entrepreneurship to writing or public speaking
- Honing your spiritual powers through regular practice of deep meditation and prayer

Doing all these things is very much like preparing a plot of land for development before you begin the architectural design of your mansion. Before you draw a single line or pour a foundation, you must have geological and hydrological surveys done, lay down sewer and water lines, build roads, grade for proper drainage, and so on. These things must all be done to support the more specific action you will take later as you design and construct your home. Since we cannot know when the hidden pattern in life will produce our sudden turn of good fortune—the inheritance, the new investor in our invention, the person who appears at just the right time—preparing our ground so that we can respond when the good fortune does appear gives us a much surer route to prosperity.

HIDDEN PATTERNS IN OTHER AREAS OF LIFE

The Law of Hidden Patterns shares a kinship with the Law of Fertility; indeed, they both deal with the idea of preparing yourself for a coming future. But where Fertility deals with the preparatory act, Hidden Patterns is about understanding that the randomness of life—as with the randomness of the stock market—is not so random after all. This invisible dynamic is critical to riding the rising tides of our times, which all who seek to be great and do great deeds for their fellows must do. We can only predict and shape our ends to a small degree; the rest is left in the hands of God and the verities of his system, and all we can do is paddle and be ready to ride the wave when it reaches the shore—or we drown beneath it.

The world is filled with hidden patterns, all of which follow the same dynamic as the stock market: apparent randomness built on a framework in which sudden shifts are inevitable. One example is the performance of sports teams, in which teams can go on sudden winning streaks for no apparent reason, dominating where they previously were also-rans. Another example is business, where competing companies or products can sell side-by-side for years before some unexplainable factor sends one of the entities soaring while the other languishes. We can apply the same principle to our health (the abrupt appearance of cancer), book sales or, most notable, the process of evolution.

In all of these areas, character and discipline become the keys to coping with the wrenching nature of sudden change, even when that change appears on the surface to be in our favor. Remember that abrupt good can be as disruptive to our Spirits as can be abrupt evil; the vital force is that of change for which we are unprepared. Society is filled with tales of heirs to great fortunes who wound up wasting every penny they inherited, committing crimes, engaging in violence against siblings who had not wasted their money, and basically ruining their lives.

When we are enlightened and use our knowledge of Spirit to shape our own characters to become individuals who look at improvements to our fortunes with gratitude and humility, we become able to leverage those improvements to lift our own situations and the situations of those around us. When we cultivate discipline and hard work at all times, even before good fortune has found us, we have the tools to multiply that fortune ten or a hundred times over by the means of our industry, innovation, and persistence. The same is true for all other hidden patterns.

THE I AM INTENTION EXISTS IN PARALLEL TO HIDDEN PATTERNS

You may have been wondering about the central tenet of New Thought—that the declaration of the I Am intention by an enlightened Spirit, followed by the individual becoming the goal in body and Mind, can manifest any desire—and where it fits in with this concept of hidden patterns. Does not the principle of I Am make randomness obsolete? Instead of waiting for things to happen and waiting for a bounce to come along and transform our fortunes, are we not instead supposed to will and envision our futures into existence?

There is no contradiction. The manifestational power of I Am and the Divine Mind exists alongside the hidden patterns of our discussion. This is possible because there are several kinds of causality in the lives of the living.

Divine influence—Here, the system of God directly manifests something into the experience of a person. These often take the form of the power of prophecy, visions, or sudden inspirations. They are unbidden and in no way can we influence or predict them.

I Am intention—As we have discussed at length, we can will new manifestations to come into our corporeal lives by casting an intention into the ether and then retaining our complete mental focus not only on the desire but on having already become the desire in our thoughts, words, and deeds. When we act wealthy, wealth comes.

Hidden pattern occurrence—The unpredictable bounce that we are discussing in this chapter comes into all lives and is the product in part of our past choices intersecting with the incomprehensibly complex patterns of human choice, natural law, and Divine manipulation. We can prepare for it but never plan for it.

Other direction—Finally, the thoughts and actions of other people shape our ends and desires. We have a great deal of control over how or if we respond to what other individuals do.

As you can see, these are all working simultaneously in every human life. So the idea that the I Am intention and hidden patterns can coexist is not surprising. While we may be exerting the force of our Minds to manifest one goal for which we have a great desire, it is not possible for any of us to know what developments will best serve our path to God's service. So, seemingly random events occur that push us in that direction, as long as we react in the appropriate way. You can think of I Am and the bounce as the active and autonomic nervous systems. Manifestation is like raising your arm—something you do consciously. The power of hidden patterns in your life is like breathing—something that goes on behind the scenes whether you think of it or not.

THE BOUNCE HIDDEN IN THE PATTERN

People usually are the bounce. Most of the time, when random events suddenly crystallize in your favor, the blessing that comes about will come to you via another person—someone temporarily anointed as a messenger of God. This is why it makes such sense to cleanse your life of toxic relationships as you prepare for the bounce. The character of the people in your circle affects the type of blessing you receive. Do you wish for the slothful, the greedy, the unfaithful, or the addicted to shape the bounty sent to you by God?

A few years back, I knew of a man, a Pentecostal minister who was a rising star in the community. This man had a crisis of conscience after a visitation from the Spirit of God, and he knew that he could no longer go on preaching the Word the way he had been—the way he had been taught. He began preaching what his conscience told him, and he was reviled as a heretic. People rarely enjoy having their views questioned. In short order, he lost his congregation, his church, his income, and very nearly his family. He was an outcast, forced to start over again.

However, because the minister was true to his principles and unafraid to share his story, his fortunes turned on a bounce. A friend told several powerful people about the man and his dramatic, courageous story. Before long, he was contacted by a literary agent about turning his experiences into several books, and ended up signing a lucrative book contract that helped him recover from his financial disaster. Now he has gained a new congregation and speaks all over the world not only about his new vision of the

Word but about tolerance of maverick ideas in the conservative religious world.

For this pastor, his friend who began making key contacts was the bounce in his life—the force that shifted his fortunes. People usually carry the blessings into your experience, which is why it pays to bless the good souls around you at all times.

Prophets Can Often Reveal Hidden Patterns

There are people who genuinely believe they can predict what will happen to you. Often, such predictions involve large sums of money and systems that promise to "beat the system." Invariably, these prove to be falsehoods. No one working with the normal five senses and the rational, linear mind can read the currents of causality and Divine nature and glean hints of what is to come.

The only individuals who can do this to some degree are the prophets. Prophecy is a Divine appointment, and there are few of us with this gift. But if you seek some kind of insight into the path your bounce might take, consult a prophet. Very often, you will not receive a direct "this is what will happen to you on this date" type of answer. As I have said, what would be the good in that? Inevitability breeds one of two reactions in humans: headlight-struck paralysis or complacency. Neither serves you nor God.

Instead, what you are most likely to receive from a prophet is a vision of what you should be doing to prepare for the bounce to come. Let's say you sit down with a proven prophet from your church and speak about the path of your life. You ask what is to come, and the prophet tells you that in order to prepare and best take advantage of the future, you should be learning a foreign language and working extra hours to save up some money. He or she has not told you what will happen, because that is probably beyond his or her ability to see clearly, and unclear information can be worse than no information at all. Instead the prophet instructs you on the ways to prepare yourself for the sudden change. This is the information that will prove most helpful.

Using this Law to your benefit and the development of your spiritual self is a matter of constancy—adhering to a code of conduct and a pattern of being that lasts for years. Spend less time worrying about what you are doing and more time paying attention to who you are becoming. That will determine much of how you benefit from the law and the inevitable bounce to come.

WHAT WE HAVE LEARNED

- Random systems are not so random; they all feature underlying patterns of sudden, positive change.

- Life is like the stock market. You cannot predict the bounce, but you can be ready to take advantage of it.

- People are the most common carriers of sudden, unpredictable blessings.

- Consistent personal growth over time is the wisest and surest way to be positioned to leverage the sudden improvement in fortune when it comes.

10

THE LAW OF HUMILITY

:: :: :: :: ::

CORE PRINCIPLES

- Temporary success can deceive the ego.

- Lack of humility equals reckless action in service of the ravenous ego.

- Only with humility can you step back from success to perceive the reason behind it.

137

I claim to be a simple individual liable to err like any other fellow mortal. I own, however, that I have humility enough to confess my errors and to retrace my steps.

—Gandhi, *The Essential Gandhi*

In the book of Daniel, King Nebuchadnezzar boasts wildly about his achievements and wealth, despite God's warning that his pride may result in his downfall. Later, the king is indeed humbled by God, who sends him into the wild to live like an animal for seven years. When Nebuchadnezzar returns, he praises God as the rightful source of all that he has. So we learn the aphorism, "Pride goeth before a fall."

Humility before God is one of humankind's noblest attributes. It acknowledges that we are not the fountain of our welfare or the makers of our lives. We are the recipients of God's largesse and should behave as such. Yet when things are going well, humility seems to elude many of us. During the last economic bubble, it was not uncommon to hear economists, investors, and corporate officers bragging about their acumen in managing assets and creating wealth.

But then we have Proverb 22:4, which says, "The reward of humility and the fear of the Lord are riches, honor and life." Doesn't the self-inflated ego of the wealthy social climber ignore that truth, hoping that wealth and riches can continue even when God turns off the flow of abundance? Yes, and events have proved that view to be demonstrably false. If there is a human failing that can be pointed to as the root cause of the economic crisis through which we have all suffered, it is pride. Don't mistake me; there is nothing wrong with pride in one's accomplishments as long as you maintain the perspective that you are achieving all by the grace of God's system and your Divine Mind.

The manifestation of riches is a direct outgrowth of the state of Mind that you maintain. A positive outlook produces positive results; a fearful Mind attracts largely objects of fear into your orbit. So, then, a prideful Mind—even if that pride stems from past spiritual successes in using the I Am intention to manifest prosperity—attracts the fruits of pride. Those are envious people, crime, resentment, and the erosion of your strengths. Pride does not go before a fall: *pride* is *the fall.*

There are two types of people in the world: those who are humble, and those who are about to be.

—Roger Lowenstein, financial journalist

HUMILITY BREEDS CHANGE

The failure of the economic meltdown was not a failure of derivatives, toxic mortgages, or banking regulation. Those were symptoms of the bigger problem. No, the recession was a failing of humility. On the institutional level, financiers and regulators assumed that they were the sources of the growth that swelled their portfolios, and they paid no heed to the truth that a boom that does not benefit all is not a boom but a bubble. The lords of Wall Street told themselves that they were the masters of economic law and that the rules were being rewritten. Magazines wrote articles about the "long boom" and how the Dow Jones average would soon top twenty thousand. There is a word for that: *hubris*, unwarranted pride leading to overreaching and downfall.

On the personal front, people just like you and me were guilty of our own lack of humility. We acquired, we paid with credit, we built up debt, we tapped the equity in our homes on the assumption that things would continue going up and up. Millions of Americans overextended ourselves because we deluded ourselves into believing that we had control. Worse, we believed that our greater financial worth meant we had greater personal worth, when personal worth comes only from being enlightened before the face of God. Wealth built through God's system is holy and elevates the Spirit; wealth built through manipulation and greed corrodes the Spirit and only makes a person mean and petty. Our petty Spirits became a petty collapse. There is a reason we call it "petty cash."

The danger of pride is that you can come to believe that you have all the answers and do not need to change or adapt. Pride leads to a sense of false self-assurance. Instead, total humility before God is the path of wisdom.

THE LAW OF HUMILITY

Being humble and aware that you are not the creator of prosperity opens you to changes that themselves foster prosperity.

The principle is beautifully illustrated by the story of a man who ran a neighborhood grocery store in a city east of Los Angeles, an area hit hard by foreclosures, where nearly 40 percent of people were at risk of losing their homes. Most of his customers were hurting as a result of bad financial decisions, and the merchant was no different; business was lagging, and he was behind on his own mortgage payments. At first, he was angry and proud and refused to ask anyone for help. He also refused to help the many people in the community who were worse off than he was. "They got themselves into this," he reasoned haughtily.

But he was also a religious man, and one night during prayer, God spoke to him and softened his heart. The next day, the merchant put a sign on his window thanking all his customers and offering one hundred dollars' worth of free items for everyone at financial risk. The line grew to extend around the block. When customers asked why he was doing this, he said, "Because I realized that all of you are the reason I have been in business for eighteen years and why I was able to buy my home." The local customers quickly picked his shelves clean. By that evening, there was nothing left. The store was empty, and the man did not know what he would do next.

But as word got out about his gesture, more affluent people from all over the region came to bring him groceries and restock his shelves. The press spread his story far and wide, and his store was packed with customers. Business improved. A local bank offered to refinance his home if he would hire a couple of local teens to help in the store, which he did. In the end, the merchant's humility saved his business, his home, and part of the spirit of his neighborhood.

Do nothing from selfishness or conceit, but in humility count others better than yourselves.

—**Philippians 2:3**

WHEN YOU ARE HUMBLE

When you are humble . . . you are quick to attribute success to those around you and to God. You realize that your responsibility is to be a worthy recipient of the Universe's generosity and to help others realize it as well.

When you are humble . . . you are not so set in your ways that you cannot change for the better. You have nothing invested in your current situation and can transform yourself in order to better serve others and share the message of enlightenments.

When you are humble . . . you are generous, because you flow with gratitude. You have the perspective to understand that for most of us abundance ebbs and flows and life comes with good times but also with tragedy. You take nothing for granted because you know that what has come to you could also be taken away.

When you are humble . . . you take steps to prevent financial disaster, because you appreciate that much of financial success has nothing to do with your brilliance. It's about luck, manipulation, or market forces far too complex to understand. So you manage your money wisely, ignore "too good to be true" offers, avoid debt, and maintain a prudent lifestyle that acknowledges that one of the greatest kinds of wealth is peace of mind.

When you are humble . . . you perceive the bubbles, swindles, and crises while others are busy predicting that they cannot happen. This prepares you for the unknown and unknowable because you do not live obliviously. You are no one's fool.

When you are humble . . . you praise and thank God in prayer or meditation. You know that he and his system are the source of all you have and that when your days here come to an end, all you have and all you are will return to God. You enter the world both rich and poor and leave this world the same way.

When you are humble ... you manifest prosperity steadily and successfully, because you know that you are not beyond the Divine demands to focus your attention on being what you desire. You maintain mental discipline and stay steadfast in your concentration, so your manifestation is powerful and blessed.

When you are humble ... you use your prosperity to help others, which in turn helps it multiply. You bring love and light to your church and community and aid others regardless of age, race, creed, or lifestyle.

The concept of humility is such a straightforward one that this chapter is not lengthy. Be mindful that he who made you is the fountainhead of all you have. In our look at prosperity, this changes slightly because we know that God's Kingdom is not heaven but his system of wealth and reward. Humility then becomes the key to making critical adjustments to your mind and actions, in order to manifest that which serves God's mission to spread enlightenment to all. The humble people will be the wealthy people because they will be unable to think only of themselves. They know that their wealth comes from all around them, from the community to the cosmos.

HUMILITY IS FOUND IN A DESIRE TO DO TRUE SERVICE

Few lie at greater risk of arrogance than the guru, teacher, or adviser. When people come to you seeking wisdom, if you don't remember that you are as dependent upon them for their faith in you as they are upon you for your words, then you will slide into hubris and fall. So a person offering financial advice, such as a stock adviser, must be a humble person—not only to avoid becoming someone who abuses his own power but to avoid placing the importance of perpetuating his own status above the importance of providing true wisdom.

How can you be humble and still position yourself as a person of wisdom, a modern-day Oracle of Delphi? By recalling that all information you share must stem from a desire for true service. If you cannot serve, then you do not advise others. The danger of having supplicants is that you will end up telling them whatever they want to hear so that they will continue to idolize you. But God casts down idols. No human is an idol—we are beings of service. If you are in a position where people come to you for stock market or other financial counsel, place your mission to serve others first above all else, including profit. Profit will come if you are centered in a humble place of service.

BE HUMBLE BEFORE MAN AND GOD

The great basketball coach John Wooden said, "Talent is God-given. Be humble. Fame is man-given. Be grateful. Conceit is self-given. Be careful."[1] We are called upon to recognize the different kinds of humility and pride and to conduct ourselves with wisdom and discretion. First, we have God-given gifts. Before God, the ultimate humility is called for. Not because we should fear punishment; God is not an archaic wounding God of the Old Testament. No, humility before God is vital because without it, we believe ourselves to be the origin of our prosperity and as such we will not spend the attention

1. http://thinkexist.com/quotation/talent_is_god_given_be_humble-fame_is_man-given/148168.html (accessed October 2009).

needed to manifest affluence with our Minds. If you don't believe in God's system, God's system will not believe in you.

Second to our fellow humans, a different humility is in order. We do not worship our brothers and sisters, but we must recognize in them the same soul-deep connection to Spirit. Being humble means respecting the truth that each person, no matter how low, possesses the same ability to touch God and to wrest wonders from the cosmos. God pressed us each out with the same power, or Divine Mind. Finally, self-humility simply means keeping the ego in check. It means having perspective: not becoming too full of pride when things go well nor too full of despair when events do not transpire in a way that is immediately beneficial to us. In truth, the wise individuals balance humility with pride that no matter what happens, their oneness with God will help them rise above.

TRAGEDY BRINGS HUMILITY FROM PRIDE

One of the most miraculous things about people is that we change. However, we do not change easily. I think this principle is best illustrated in the biography of ex-gangster Arthur Powell, which he makes available online under his company title E.G.R.E.S.S Consultants, Inc.:

[Arthur Powell] became exposed to the criminal elements of the streets at the early age of 13. By age 15, he was involved with neighborhood cliques, which later became recognized as "gangs." When Arthur (street name "Art") was 19 he met a drug dealer who took him under his wing and gave him power to terrify anyone who was against their family (gang), which was called "I Refuse Posse." From the years of 1988–1992, I Refuse Posse reigned terror on the streets of Atlanta. Arthur was a major

contributor to much of the gang violence that took place in Atlanta. In 1993, his criminal activity finally sent him to prison for 11 years and 6 months.

While incarcerated, Arthur changed mentally and spiritually. He pledged to dedicate his life to helping to keep the youth out of gangs. Considering Arthur's affiliation with gangs in the past and having first-hand experience of serving a lengthy prison term, he offers a magnitude of insight into the world of youth violence, street life, and provides solutions to prevent criminal and gang activities.

Arthur is now a Gang Prevention Expert/Life Skills Coach and has started his own company, E.G.R.E.S.S. Consultants, Inc. E.G.R.E.S.S. is an acronym for Ex Gangsta Reviewing Experiences Suffered in Surroundings.[2]

Tragedy can be a great blessing when it sparks the wisdom in us to know that humility is the only road to total communion with God and unity with our fellow men. We are nothing alone.

THE VALUE OF PRIDE IN STARTING A BUSINESS

You might think that pride would be of the most use when seeking employment, but that is rarely the case. Employers are usually in need of people who work well with others and who share credit for their achievements. Excessive boasting at an interview is a sure way to find yourself thanked politely and then dismissed.

However, launching any kind of new enterprise (including a church) can be such a grueling affair that it does pay to have some

---

2. http://egressconsultants.com (accessed November 2009).

level of pride. You see, such an endeavor usually involves original thinking, and there are people who think original thinking is inevitably doomed to failure. Innovators and naysayers run in pairs through the economic savannah; where you find one person saying, "What if?" you will find at least one other saying, "It won't work!" It takes pride to resist such negative thinking, for the entrepreneur to keep faith and will a new business into existence.

With this pride, of course, must be humility in equal measure. No entrepreneur can open his or her doors with a gust of arrogance—the sense that the market "cannot live without what I have to offer." That is a sure way to fail. Instead, pride in your idea must be balanced with the humility that your mission is to serve.

You know whether you are prideful or humble. If you are prideful, it is vital that you know the ways in which pride has tripped you up in the past. If you are humble, it is equally vital that you understand how to let that humility drive your perspective and personal change as you bring prosperity into your life and the lives of others.

WHAT WE HAVE LEARNED

- Excessive pride leads to overreaching and disaster.

- Humility before God is wisdom.

- The humble person has perspective and foresight.

- Humility and service go together.

11

THE LAW OF INVESTMENT

▪   ▪   ▪   ▪   ▪

┌─────────────── CORE PRINCIPLES ───────────────┐

- If you want to reverse your fortunes, first reverse your thinking.

- You must think in ways that represent prudent risk.

- Right thinking today produces results not today but in the future.

└──┘

The real source of wealth and capital in this new era is not material things ... it is the human mind, the human spirit, the human imagination, and our faith in the future.

—Steve Forbes

When times are hard and it seems that ill fortune is all that is in store, it is easy to slide down the slope into habitual negative thinking. It becomes very easy to think only about today and fall into a common failing of human cognition: believing that the way things are today is the way they will always be. That kind of thinking is extremely hazardous because it distorts our thought. What experts call the *recency bias* led to the economic bubble, in which millions believed that real estate values and incomes would somehow go up forever. The same flaw in logic (a derivation of the word *logos*, or "thought") leads to depression and resignation when hard times come. We begin to believe that things will never change—that they *cannot* change.

Recency bias means that we are predisposed to think that things will not change, despite evidence to the contrary. This is a consequence in part of our baser material nature—not perceiving the grand sweep of time as it flows in all directions. Despite the fact that recent laboratory experiments in quantum mechanics have revealed that time indeed flows forward and backward simultaneously (and, in fact, what we call "time" may actually be an illusion created by our primitive brains), for the most part we are doomed to perceive time as only going forward and being a static force. Not being able to perceive time as a fluid, dynamic system, we do not see that change is constant and inevitable; current conditions cannot remain as they are in the physical world. Only in the realm of Spirit do things not decay, die, evolve, and transform.

Yet we cannot easily believe this. It is a natural human habit, it seems, to believe that the old rule that all things must change does not apply to us. Indeed, the great Sir John Templeton, the investment guru and spiritual pioneer, whose Templeton Prize encourages research into the connection between science and religion, said, "The four most dangerous words in investing are 'This time it's different.'" Our Minds, Divine though they may be in origin, fall into this trap constantly. Rather than invest in our futures through prosperous thought, we wallow in the unhappy present and therefore reap poverty in the future.

Goodness is the only investment that never fails.
—Henry David Thoreau, *Walden*, Vol. 2

INVESTING WITH MONEY OR MIND

The concept of investment is an ancient one: putting away small amounts of money over a long period of time to fund a venture that carries with it a manageable element of risk. The greater the risk, the greater the potential of loss, but also the greater potential of reward. The key factor is that investing must be done with a vision for the future, not the present; the act is designed to pay dividends many years hence, not today. Therefore, the act of investment is a Divine extension of our limited material Mind forward in time, bringing us more into harmony with the Divine nature of our beings.

As we have discussed many times, thought is the true currency of God's economy, not money. Money is merely thought made material, able to be exchanged between those who are enlightened and those who are not. But for the enlightened, thought is the purest force able to bring about change and to attract prosperity into our corporeal sphere. When we invest with our Minds, we are placing thoughts into the ether to begin forming future results in our conscious experience. The nature of those results depends on the nature of our thoughts: prosperous, productive, and rich thoughts breed future returns of wealth, happiness, and plenty, while thoughts that dwell on poverty, sadness, and resentment produce more poverty and misery.

The Law of Investment

Just as money breeds money, thoughts of prosperity breed the future certainty of prosperity, so you must invest in your future with prosperous thinking today.

In essence, the Law is a warning against "irrational pessimism" (the flip side of Alan Greenspan's "irrational exuberance"). If you dwell on misfortunes in your economic life, such as a job layoff or a bankruptcy, you make investments with those thoughts into the account of your future manifestation. Instead, it is far more in your interest to forcefully thrust your Mind from contemplation of miseries and into the forthright consideration and envisioning of a more prosperous future.

Example: You are one of the millions to lose your job this year. You find that you cannot escape the feelings of anger and panic that come with your loss of income, so you indulge yourself and wallow in them for months. As a result, many things occur:

1. You cripple your immediate life by poisoning it with rage and resentment.

2. You harm your ability to find a new job and pull yourself out of your current situation.

3. You project unintentional but powerful chords of pain and poverty into the psychoreactive substance of the cosmos, setting off an eventual return reaction of the same into your life.

The third result is by far the most dangerous. The Universe is made of Consciousness and reacts to Consciousness. This is similar to the physics principle that for each action there is an equal and opposite reaction, except that for each thought you project into the cosmic Consciousness, the same type of thought is reflected back to you as physical experience. This is why I refer to thoughts as "thought investments"; they deliver a return that matches what and how wisely you have invested. When you invest anger and pervasive thoughts of poverty into the Universe, eventually your investment return will be anger- and poverty-related material experiences: the loss of another job, a lawsuit, retribution by a creditor, or some other misfortune.

TAKE CONTROL AND PROJECT FORWARD

Now, take another example of mental investment. The same event sparks the chain of events: you lose your job through no fault of your own. But instead of dwelling on anger or fear, you make a conscious decision to wrest your Mind from the pain of the present and project it into the future. You forcibly turn your thinking to opportunity, hope, creation, and abundance, knowing that these things may not be present in the moment but that by consistently broadcasting them into the etheric plane, you will bring them to you in material form in your future.

Have Mercy upon me, O Lord, Sustainer of the world. The dust of the feet of the Saints is all the treasure I need. In the Company of the True Guru, one's investment remains intact.

—**Shri Guru Granth Sahib**

There is vast power in such investment. It is the hallmark of all Divine action; Jesus did it when he predicted his own return after death, and Moses did it when he led the Hebrews out of bondage into the unknown. A truly evolved and Spirit-connected Mind teaches itself to escape the chains of the now and focus attention on the to-come, knowing that now is already done and cannot be changed. So why dwell upon it? The inherent self-pity and futility of regret and rage are utterly self-defeating. When you transcend time and cast your perception into tomorrow with thoughts of the good and wealth that are sure to come, you produce a new set of outcomes:

1. The immediate present becomes more bearable and relationships remain strong.

2. You are empowered to take action to change your current circumstances, and your positive state of mind inspires others to want to assist you.

3. After a time, you begin to see the return on your mental investment in the form of new opportunity, sacred new relationships,
partners who come into your life to bring your projects exactly
what they need, financial windfalls, and so on.

How long does this sort of return on investment take? That is
one question no one can answer. Even God could not reveal it to
you if he chose to, for the mechanics of the return on mental investment are dictated by the infinitely subtle workings of God's system.
This is why it pays to guard your thoughts and, as much as possible,
endeavor to train your Mind to project energies of hope, positivity,
and prosperity into the cosmos. Every word has power.[1] Such
thought investment could bear fruit in six months or thirty years.
This is what the biblical phrase "thou knowest not the day nor the
hour" refers to—not to some mythical apocalypse but to the response
from the Universe to the energies of your mind. It is impossible to
predict when your thoughts will come back to you, so it is best to be
wary and maintain a disciplined Mind rooted in the hope of Spirit
and trust in God.

I love the thinking of Jewish scholar Steven Schwarzman about
the subject of investment. In part, he writes:

> The traditional count of 613 commandments means that there
> are that many ways for us to connect to our Jewish selves—and
> to our ancestors and other Jews today. There may be no tax
> advantages to a 613(k) plan, but the long-term value is clear.
> Start making small daily, weekly and monthly time invest-
> ments in growing as a person and as a Jew. Often we are just

---

1. "Every word has power" refers to the book *Every Word Has Power*, by Yvonne Oswald (Hillsboro,
OR: Atria Books/Beyond Words Publishing, 2008).

reciting how returning to our true selves, talking frankly with God in prayer and speaking to the people around us in this world through acts of righteousness can annul the severity of our decree for the coming year—the traditional formulation in the mahzor noting that while we are judged for our sins, we are nonetheless given the benefit of God's mercy when we engage in the right kind of behavior.[2]

Concentration on long-term growth rather than short-term gain is indicative of the spiritually advanced individual. Small investments in growth and positive motion produce positive and fruitful thinking—precisely the kind of thought patterns that reverberate back upon the thinker with greater riches, increased opportunity, and enhanced creativity and innovation.

You Cannot Predict the Return on Thought Investment

The thoughts that you project from your Divine Mind into the world of Spirit are not analogous to what you receive in return, because your investments pay off in the material, not the spiritual. It's a bit like investing money in the stock market and when the time comes to retire and take the money out, instead of cash you receive a house. Not bad, but perhaps not what you were fully prepared to leverage.

Mental projections provoke a kind of reaction from the etheric plane, but they have no precise predictive power; that is, projecting anger after a job loss does not guarantee that you will later be con-

---

2. Steven Schwarzman, "Rebalancing Our Spiritual Portfolios," *Jewish Review*, http://www.jewish review.org/money/Rebalancing-our-spiritual-portfolios (accessed October 2009).

fronted by an angry person who will attack you. There is no way of knowing exactly how your thought investment will manifest down the line. However, the sacred wisdom of the Prophet tells us that what ye sow, so shall ye reap, so you can expect a return of the same tenor as your invested mental state.

So pervasive thoughts of panic—a chaotic mental state—are likely to bring material results that also represent chaos: family unrest, violence, a lawsuit being filed against you. Thoughts of anger and resentment are likely to manifest in the future as betrayal by confidantes, infidelity by others, criminal activity, or theft. By the same token, continuous attention to abundance is more likely to return financial good fortune and an influx of creative and profitable ideas, while a mind-set anchored in hope and gratitude reflects back on the Mind as an end to conflict, the appearance of allies, generosity by others, or the discovery of great value. The key is that there is no way to predict these specific results or their natures. This means that we must not only be on guard to project positive thoughts but be creative and open as to how we greet and use their corporeal manifestations.

SOME THOUGHTS PRESENT
MORE RISK THAN OTHERS

As we have discussed, the rate of return on an investment depends on the level of risk involved. The greater the risk, the greater the potential reward, but also the higher the possibility of total loss. The amount of risk is up to the individual choice of each person. We all possess the total freedom to select our own path and our own state of personal evolution. But it is vital to understand that the greater risk you take to your own present comfort, the greater reward you will enjoy.

That means that the more effort you undertake to grow beyond your current state of spiritual maturity in both thought and action, which will enable you to better serve God's purpose, the richer your results will be. We see this when we observe the lives of prophets and others who have surrendered all their worldly means of support in order to become perfect vessels for God's will. The more they peel away the layers of their old lives and rely only on God's system to produce their bread and wine, the greater the miracles that manifest in their lives. You do not have to be a martyr or prophet, but know that the further you step away from the stream of your current life in order to become the being God wants you to be, the more plentiful the riches you will receive.

Here is an example of a "curve of spiritual risk" and the rewards each presents:

Little risk: Investing in thoughts of plenty when you are already affluent or moderately comfortable. Result: Little to no change in the state of your being and little manifestation in your future.

Moderate risk: Investing thoughts and actions toward starting your own church when you are modestly middle class and have never launched an organization before. Result: Solid material manifestations and the development of greater spiritual wisdom and knowledge.

Great risk: Giving away most of your material possessions when you are affluent with the goal of purifying yourself and gaining enlightenment. Result: Dramatic manifestations of personal enlightenment, financial opportunity, and incredible relationships.

Degree of risk is a personal choice. But the more you can rely on God and leave the center of your comfortable, predictable existence with the intent of evolving into the being he intended you to be, the vastly richer your results will be. Risk is worthwhile as long as you undertake it honestly.

Perfect Compliance Is Not Required to Realize Full Returns from Thought

No one can maintain perfectly disciplined thoughts at all times. The most spiritual among us lapses into thoughts of sloth, greed, despair, or apathy. Even Jesus lost faith and asked his father to take the cup from his lips. God understands that as corporeal beings we are not perfect and are subject to the effects of the events and people around us, so he built his cosmic economic system to account for this.

For this reason, it is not necessary to be flawless in thought in order to realize the best return on investment. If that were the case, no one, not even the finest masters of spiritual discipline, would ever manifest wealth or opportunity, because being human means failing, being imperfect, being subject to distraction and temptation. But we do realize the returns on our mental discipline; we do produce wonders out of the etheric state of being and change the world. So clearly, perfection is not needed for production. Flawlessness does not precede progress.

No, instead, all that God's system asks is a consistent flow of prosperous, positive mental energies to activate the mechanisms that convey blessings to us. If your general state of mind is positive and affirmative throughout the day, with periods of intense concentration on prosperous and positive thoughts, that is enough to activate the Divine machine that brings forth blessings in the form of material experience. Similarly, a concentration on the good and hopeful cancels out periodic lapses into sadness, self-pity, or thoughts of desperation or the sureness of lingering poverty. In a way, intense mental focus on an I Am intention of wealth and opportunity can inoculate you against incoming negative results.

This dynamic operates in much the same way as financial investing. A few bad financial decisions do not doom you to losing your principal as long as your fundamental underlying strategy is sound and steady. You need not police your thinking every minute of the day in order to be assured of bringing forth healthy returns from your thought investment. The scale simply needs to balance strongly toward the positive.

WE ARE GOD'S THOUGHT INVESTMENT

God understands the significance of risk and reward, and his awareness informs his choice to create humans as creatures capable of great folly as well as great wonder and courage. In birthing us to fill his own need to operate in the world of flesh, God made a risky investment in our existence. But this risk was needed in order for God to realize the ultimate return on investment: the evolution of a higher, more enlightened cosmos.

We are the tools and proxies of God's intent in the tangible world. But why would a perfect being not create perfect tools? Because that which is perfect does not evolve and learn from its mistakes. God wanted beings who would become aware of their own shortfalls and choose to rise above them, as human beings often choose to do. This effort and struggle is what makes us so creative in finding new ways to better ourselves—it is the birth of the entrepreneurial impulse in humankind. God invests his thought in us, not knowing if any individual will prove out his or her total potential but with the certainty that some individuals will choose to become enlightened.

So be of good cheer. God has made an investment in you with the surety that you will succeed and return wonders. All you must do is fulfill the potential he has already placed within you.

TO OVERTURN MISFORTUNE, INVEST IN THOUGHTS THAT ALIGN WITH YOUR PASSION

The purpose to which you are drawn is the fulcrum on which your thought investment should turn. This is not just about generic positive thoughts; there should be direction behind your intention, and the surest way to produce it is through following your passion. If you have a passion to start a business, yet face an economic setback, the surest way to turn it around is to do the following:

1. Force your mind away from thoughts of the negative present and set it on your goal.

2. Set forth an intention in your mind to become the essence of that goal.

3. Maintain the core thoughts and emotional impressions of that intention—courage, hope, charity, a creative business idea—in your mind as often as possible during your waking hours.

4. Concentrate only on the manifestation of those thoughts and feelings during at least two hours of daily prayer and meditation.

5. Have faith and trust that God's system will return your investment to you.

This process will see results and you will experience them in your material life.

■ ■ ■ ■ ■

Using this Law is a matter of personal discipline and mental control. It may not seem fair that our thoughts can come back to haunt us, but that is the system that God has created; in reality, our thoughts and words are who we are, so why should our lives not reflect our beings? Find the power to control and command your thoughts out of the present darkness and into future light, and that light shall be yours.

WHAT WE HAVE LEARNED

- The Mind tends toward the present.

- You must forcibly evict yourself from focus on the present and lock your thoughts on a better future.

- The riskier your thoughts—the more they take you out of your comfort zone—the greater the return.

- You are God's thought investment.

12

THE LAW OF
MENTAL CAPITAL

■ ■ ■ ■ ■

CORE PRINCIPLES

- You are a source of wealth for others.

- Creating wealth in others enriches the human ecosystem and sustains your own wealth.

- You share mental capital by inspiring others.

Thought, not money, is the real business capital.

—Harvey S. Firestone, American industrialist

Entrepreneur, TV personality, and fashion designer Jen Groover, author of the book *What If and Why Not?*, believes that as an entrepreneur and spiritual person, her role is to use her ideas not only to build her own fortunes, but to create jobs and prosperity for others. This position shows a keen understanding of one of the fundamental facts about God's economy: thought is capital best used when it is working and flexing its muscles in the community, coming to life for many people.

Each of us is a storehouse of mental capital: ideas, inspiration, and wisdom with the potential to create economic and financial wealth. You may have an idea for a product, while a fellow member of your congregation has the management knowledge to get that product to market, and still another has experience from years in business to warn you of potential pitfalls. The point is that our mental capital is not designed to be hoarded for the benefit of any one individual. We fulfill our highest sacred destiny when we use the prosperity-creating might of our Minds to enrich not only ourselves but to give others the means to generate their own world-changing prosperity.

Take the hip-hop impresario Jay-Z as an example. He may have started out as just another rapper and musician, but he quickly became a mogul and helped to bring African American urban culture to the commercial forefront. As a result, his ideas and innovations have created an industry that employs hundreds of thousands of people and has in turn inspired others to launch their own musical and entrepreneurial careers. Like my good and godly brother Russell Simmons, Jay-Z has leveraged his mental capital to enrich not only himself but an entire world.

Capital as such is not evil; it is its wrong use that is evil. Capital in some form or other will always be needed.
—Gandhi, *The Encyclopaedia of Gandhian Thoughts*

GOD, CAPITALIST

What is capital but the power of creation? Capital is simply that which is invested to create greater wealth. Now, in traditional terms, that's money: you get a business loan and invest that capital in starting a company with the intention of making more money. But money is just thought in material form—the power to move and direct the actions of others. So Mind is the true capital. And what is capital used for but creation and expansion? Those are the fundamental purposes of life and Mind and Spirit. God created the cosmos and its laws, and the purpose of humanity and the cosmic Consciousness is to expand the will of God throughout the material realm and eventually unite matter and Spirit as one. If capitalism is the creation of things that did not exist until they came into being in the Mind of a being, then God is a capitalist.

Use that as a foil to anyone who takes you to task for the Prosperity Gospel and insists that holiness means poverty. God was the first capitalist: he conceived of the material cosmos in his Consciousness, and indeed conceived of us the same way, embedding us in that same universal Consciousness. This was the universe brought into being. How is that any different from a young man like Mark Zuckerberg conceiving one day of a website that would allow college students to connect with one another from anywhere in the world, then making that vision a reality? By the way, Zuckerberg's idea has become Facebook, which you may have heard of. The act of creation is an act of entrepreneurship—the conception and manifestation of something that did not exist before.

So it is not a great leap to see that your Mind and ideas and concepts are capital in the same way that God's are. We already know that we are all intimately, eternally intertwined with the Mind of God; we are God pressed out from Spirit into flesh, and we possess the same gifts of envisioning and manifestation as does God. Your mental capital—your notion for an invention, your original song, your knowledge of how to build a custom home—is an act of creation waiting to be born. It is a Divine power that you possess, and all the more so when you employ it to benefit others as well as yourself. Creation is outward-driven, not inward-driven. We create first to satisfy our passion, but then we project our creation outward to touch others.

THE LAW OF MENTAL CAPITAL

You will gain when you allow other people to tap the power of your Mind for their benefit.

Creators have the duty to be generous with their visions, and doing so is indeed in their benefit. Consider someone like film director Peter Jackson, who made the blockbuster *Lord of the Rings* films. Given the responsibility of spending $300 million to produce a film trilogy of perhaps the most beloved work of fiction of all time, he did not become a dictator. He famously gave his crews and creative staff autonomy so long as they kept his central vision in mind. The result was that an army of creative professionals enhanced Jackson's central vision with a vision of their own and a masterpiece was crafted.

Or consider the urban dweller who decides to start her own clothing line. At first, everything is about her; after all, she must find the startup funds, create the designs, do all the work, and make the sales. But if she is wise and shares her ideas and vision with others, her world expands. If she hires people and mentors them, she brings money to the community and helps foster future entrepreneurs. If she shares her vision with other businesspeople, she may find partners or investors, or inspire others to emulate what she is doing. Perhaps she advises a local high school club on how to create its own T-shirts as a fundraiser or becomes a philanthropist supporting a campaign to end homelessness. Her mental capital has reached out and enhanced the lives of many, many others beyond the limited scope of her company. And her company is stronger for it.

> *Capital is that part of wealth which is devoted to obtaining further* x
> *wealth.*
>
> —**Alfred Marshall**, *The Economics of Industry*

Ways to Share Your Mental Capital

Your ideas and visions should, of course, first be applied to benefit you and yours. We are the captains of our own souls. However, that is a short-lived thing, as is a plant in water without soil. When you allow others to tap your mental capital to create their own prosperity, you launch a cascade of unpredictable but wondrous benefits for yourself as well. The winding ways of Consciousness and human relations are complex and hard to predict, but inevitably, when you become the source for the good of many others, you will become far richer for it.

Take the example of the teacher in a Chicago public school several decades ago. Too busy to write books himself, he nonetheless had many wonderful ideas for both novels and nonfiction books, which he passed along to his students with only the proviso that if any of them ever turned his ideas into books, they should thank him in the acknowledgments. He never thought anything more of it; it was a natural act of generosity—a recognition of the truth that an idea kept isolated from the light of other Minds withers like a flower denied the sun. He probably assumed no one would ever do anything with his ideas.

He was wrong. Apparently, he was quite an inspiring teacher because more than ten of his students actually published books based on the ideas they got from him, and all credited him in their works. This would be a heartwarming story had it ended there, but it did not. Fast forward thirty years and—due to budget cuts and teacher layoffs—the school where this beloved man, now in his sixties, teaches was threatened with closure. But at the last minute, several of his former students rode to the rescue—the ones who had written bestselling books based on the ideas he had given them. They donated a substantial amount of money themselves and organized a fund-raiser to find matching funds, and the school was saved. All this because one man decided not to hoard his mental capital but to share it—to sow it like seeds on the wind—and let it blossom.

There are many ways to use your mental capital for your own benefit and that of others:

Mentoring—A saying goes that a mentor is someone whose hindsight becomes your foresight. Mentoring is the act of fostering the development of someone else's knowledge in an area in which you have experience. Great mentors are crucial to schools, businesses, the arts, politics ... virtually *every endeavor of life*. By becoming a mentor, you typically take a younger or less experienced person under your wing and give the benefit of your experience and accumulated knowledge to help them avoid errors and make better judgments. A mentor is in a position of trust that can shape the lives of both mentor and mentee for the better. By sharing your mental capital in this way, you are going the "teach a man to fish" route: imparting knowledge that will make the less experienced person wiser and more capable. Best of all, those who are mentored are more likely to go on and become mentors themselves.

Hiring—Very simply, you start a business and eventually you hire some people to help you run it. But this is much more than that. When you hire workers from the community, you're not just providing a salary. You are giving people direction and pride, sharing your knowledge on how to do things, and helping stimulate the local material economy. Very often, hiring people of character and drive leads to decades-long relationships in which your employees become longtime allies, partners, and even co-owners ... or go on to use what they have learned and launch their own companies. All employers should encourage their people to learn all they can and then leave to start their own enterprises, because this greatly enriches local life and the local economy.

Teaching—Whether you're teaching business or finance at a college, or teaching young people or single mothers how to sew clothing or do word processing at a job center, teaching is the most direct way to pass on your mental capital to as large a group as possible.

While mentoring tends to be one-on-one, teaching can be one-on-one-hundred, a ratio that allows your knowledge to deliver the greatest possible impact. When you put your mental capital to work in the minds of others as a teacher, you gain in many ways: greater respect in the community, job security and increased pay, and a healthier, happier local environment for you and your loved ones. Teaching is among the noblest of occupations.

Incubating—Helping others bring their business ideas to life, so-called incubators are simply environments where entrepreneurs come together with mentors and resources to turn their ideas into companies. The famous Idealab in Pasadena, California, is one; the online Launcher's Café is another. The objective is the same—to give would-be entrepreneurs feedback and advice on how to refine their ideas and get them off the ground. What a wonderful and Divine way to pass on mental capital, by assisting others in using their abilities as creators. You might benefit by becoming an investor in some of these companies, finding new opportunities, or even getting an idea you can use in your own business.

ACTIVITIES AS MENTAL CAPITAL

The British government has gotten wind of the concept of mental capital and its importance for the well-being of body and Spirit. A think tank called Foresight produced a comprehensive study of the subject:

> *[The] Mental Capital and Wellbeing report, which was compiled by more than 400 scientists, proposes a campaign modeled on the nutrition initiative, to encourage behavior that will make people feel better about themselves. People should try to*

*connect with others, to be active, to take notice of their sur-
roundings, to keep learning, and to give to their neighbors and
communities ... The project investigated ways of improving the
nation's "mental capital," which Professor John Beddington
likened to a bank account of the mind. "We need to ask what
actions can add to that bank account, and what activities can
erode that capital," he said.*[1]

This validation of the idea is valuable and exciting because
it demonstrates that we are on the right track with our ideas for
self-enlightenment.

My writing of this book is an act of mental capitalism because I
am sharing my insight and prophetic knowledge with you in an
attempt to help you become more prosperous. That is the bench-
mark you must look to achieve; is your action designed to share
knowledge or wisdom that helps someone else become more prosperous? It does not matter if it is also self-serving to some degree;
good deeds are often self-serving. What matters is that you leverage your God-given knowledge in order to enlighten the Mind
of another.

From this perspective, several other types of activity can be considered mental capitalism. Charity work such as helping addicts end
their substance abuse habits can fall under this umbrella, because
the knowledge that you share will aid them in improving their lives
and becoming more prosperous. Ministering can also be seen as
capitalistic, because the information and wisdom you share about
God and his system are designed to help others take full advantage

---

1. Mark Henderson, "Do Five Simple Things a Day to Stay Sane, Say Scientists," *The Times* (London),
October 22, 2008, http://www.timesonline.co.uk/tol/life_and_style/health/mental_health/
article4988978.ece (accessed October 2009).

of that system, becoming more prosperous and happier in the long run. Even parenting, the ultimate and most important duty in the world, is a capitalist venture. You constantly pass on all your accumulated wisdom, lessons, hard experiences, and discoveries to make your children as deep in character and as self-contained as you can before they venture into the world. I can think of nothing more based on mental capital.

Activities that are designed not to teach but to lecture are not capitalistic. When you make someone else dependent on you for their prosperity, you are not sharing mental capital. You are stunting the spiritual development of another and hampering your own future potential as well.

BENEFIT FROM YOUR SHARED MENTAL CAPITAL

Make no mistake, pure altruism is not required to be a good steward of mental capital. Remember, God wants you to be prosperous, rich, and live in a fine mansion. The wealthy are those who provoke meaningful change. The poor have no power. So, there is nothing in the system that suggests sharing of mental capital must be done with only the needs of others in mind. Ideally, your benefit and the benefits of other people are coequal. In the end, you benefit in two important ways when you freely and openly share your knowledge, ideas, brainstorms, visions, and hard-earned experience.

First, you benefit financially, because by planting your knowledge in the minds of many others and sending it into the world to grow, you multiply your knowledge. Ideas can come back to you as inventions, students can return as partners, contacts can become key investors, and your largesse can build you a network of grateful individuals who wish to help you in any way they can, from referring business to offering lower cost professional services. There are so many ways to benefit financially from the selfless sharing of information that it ceases to be selfless, but enlightened self-interest is very much sacred in the Mind of God. It is how we better ourselves so that we can better others.

Second, you benefit from deeper, richer relationships with individuals and the community. Your standing in the community is enhanced, your reputation elevated, and your goodwill marked by others. Being perceived as a fount of worthwhile knowledge and generosity enriches your personal and professional interactions with everyone you meet. You may also play a role in improving your community by fostering the economic improvement of others, making your entire sphere more prosperous, better educated, more self-loving, and more able to serve the purpose of the Almighty. Rich reward indeed.

WHAT NOT TO SHARE AS PART OF MENTAL CAPITAL

There is such a thing as too much information. As the great Kahlil Gibran said, "If you reveal your secrets to the wind you should not blame the wind for revealing them to the trees."[2] The unspoken truth about mental capital is that it is about sharing information that is of value to the people who are coming to you for knowledge. Business ideas, life wisdom, how-to instructions, advice on personal improvement—these are some of the very valid areas in which mental capital applies. Others, however, should not be part of that dynamic:

---

2. http://thinkexist.com/quotation/if_you_reveal_your_secrets_to_the_world_you_should/15674.html (accessed October 2009).

Personal secrets—Private information, such as the affairs between a husband and wife, are no one else's business unless you are expressly in the business of counseling people on marriage or relationships. Even then, it is wiser to use general examples rather than sharing deeply personal information that could prove humiliating or painful to someone else.

Gossip—Bertrand Russell said, "No one gossips about other people's secret virtues."[3] Gossip is more than falsehood, it is venomous exaggeration compounded by malice and ignorance. It can damage relationships, destroy friendships, and wreck credibility. If you pass along gossip, you may soon find yourself cut off from the flow of all information because no one feels he or she can trust you.

Sworn secrets—Do not break a vow of confidentiality in order to share information with someone, no matter what the circumstances. First, you may be under legal prohibition, and if you reveal facts you have sworn to keep secret, you may find yourself standing before an earthly judge. Second, violating personal confidences has the same corrosive effect as gossip: no one will trust you.

Falsehoods—The boy who cried wolf was eventually eaten because his credibility had dwindled to nothing due to repeated lying. There are two kinds of falsehood to avoid passing along as mental capital. The first is false information that you know to be false but share because you want to impress people. The second is

---

3. Bertrand Russell, *The Basic Writings of Bertrand Russell* (Philadelphia, PA: Taylor & Francis, 2009), 403.

false information that is hearsay but you share despite knowing that it is of a dubious nature. Neither should be shared; both will damage your reputation as a source of reliable information.

Unwise advice—Giving others counsel on choices that are unsafe, unlawful, or unethical is always unwise. Your guiding star as a mental capitalist should always be to pass along wisdom and guidance to live a life in accordance with spiritual values and with lawful conduct that benefits the community.

REQUESTING SOMEONE ELSE'S MENTAL CAPITAL IS AN HONOR

If you are in the position of seeking someone else's ideas or knowledge, do not become a supplicant on your hands and knees. It is not warranted. Keep in mind that to be asked by another to share what he or she knows is a great honor; you are offering a show of great respect and love for that other person's learning and experience. When you encounter someone with knowledge that could benefit you, simply make a respectful request and remind the individual that what you will learn you will pass along—if not in specific information then in the act of mentoring and being a mental capitalist yourself.

If the party in question is an enlightened being, you will not need to do more than ask. Anyone with an open Spirit and a fertile Mind will instantly grasp the value of seeding the world with his or her ideas and creativity and will agree to teach you. This can be a wonderful path for escaping economic misfortune: sitting at the feet of someone who has made her own great success and discovering her secrets. Then you must follow through, and that is an act of will that only you can undertake.

Ideas and Knowledge
Not Shared Will Rot

Knowledge is meant to be free in the street to find its own home in multiple Minds. It is not meant to be hoarded any more than money is. Money kept in a mattress will not grow but will gradually lose much of its value; ideas kept locked away, whether out of fear, jealousy, or laziness, will decay. All knowledge needs an influx of fresh expression and exposure to the light of radical ideas in order to continue blooming. If you sit on your knowledge and experience, it will fester in you and harm your manifestation.

Make an effort to share what you have learned as a deliberate part of your personal and spiritual success strategy; do not wait for someone else to come and ask you.

The Law of Mental Capital is among the most cherished of these laws because it offers hope to those in need of a path out of economic hardship. Those who have knowledge can stimulate the "manifestation engine" of the cosmos by spreading their information into the community and creating a network of people who admire and will assist them. Those who need knowledge can learn from those who have it and go on to create new prosperity and, in turn, pass on what they have learned to others. As long as the sharing of mental capital is done with honesty, ethics, legality, and an eye to always elevating the other, it is a pure blessing.

WHAT WE HAVE LEARNED

- Mental capital is the power of creation.

- God is a capitalist who wants you to be rich.

- There are some things that should not be shared: gossip, lies, etc.

- You will always benefit from sharing mental capital with others.

13

THE LAW OF OBSTACLES

■ ■ ■ ■ ■

CORE PRINCIPLES

- Failure is God's testing ground.

- Obstacles measure your ability to grow.

- Severe failures often precede coming riches.

Obstacles cannot crush me. Every obstacle yields to stern resolve. He who is fixed to a star does not change his mind.

—Leonardo da Vinci

Helplessness is not something that comes naturally. Certainly circumstances can impose it upon us, as has occurred with many in difficult economic times, but often helplessness and failure are not facts but choices made by us as conscious beings. The idea of self-esteem often comes into play, but the source of self-love is frequently misunderstood by parents, educators, and clergy. Self-esteem does not stem from being given things to fool your Mind into feelings of achievement. It stems from overcoming obstacles to achieve a goal, and dealing with failure along the way.

Unless human beings face obstacles in life, our will atrophies. A paucity of failure and struggle is tolerable as long as life proceeds without any reversal or tragedy. But how often does life do that? Never. Life is struggle, work, and overcoming barriers. Those actions build and strengthen the "muscles" of will, discipline, and faith. Otherwise, we end up with a scenario like this: we graduate from school and enter the job market believing that we are entitled to a good job with great pay and health benefits. Why? Because circumstances have taught us that good things are simply there for the taking. When we discover that we cannot simply order up our version of reality, feelings of helplessness can set in and self-reinforce.

The Law of this chapter deals with the necessity for hard times. Like millions of Americans, you may be experiencing such times right now. If you are, you may be thinking that such economic duress—having little or no income, facing debt, possibly confronting foreclosure—can hardly be considered a blessing. But that is not what I'm saying. What I'm saying is that such times are necessary for us to grow toward enlightenment. We are not beings who operate at our highest when we are living easy, when the "fish are jumpin' and the cotton is high." The reason is a fundamental conflict between our Divine origins and our material reality.

One of the most pernicious diseases of humankind is complacency, the tendency to grasp at the delusion that "everything is fine" when in fact we might be facing financial disaster, courting a heart attack because of excessive weight, on the cusp of a failed marriage, or a hundred other disasters. We are highly skilled at finding the low level of tolerability in a situation and then inflating it to grand proportions while simultaneously screening out all evidence that we are on the road to ruin. We do this because while our inherently Divine nature grants us the theoretical ability to order our reality with mental intention, this is not something we simply wake up with the ability to do. It must be learned and developed as any skill is. We possess a Spirit memory of our Divine nature, and some of us crave that power without paying the price to get it. Unless we make a conscious decision to develop our I Am intention and to hone the ability to manifest our thought, some of us settle for the pale substitute: self-delusion.

The presence of obstacles in our lives is a natural outgrowth of the psychoreactive nature of the cosmos. God does not want us to struggle; in a purely Spirit universe, he would have us have all we desire. However, because he created us to function in the material world, he knows that cannot be the case. If we are to evolve and learn and grow into his purpose, we must do so by being shocked out of the illusion that, to put it simply, "wishing can make it so." So, God created a system in which all beings, whether enlightened or not, forever project our thoughts into the ether and produce manifestations. Those people who are troubled, tormented, or self-deluding, though they might tell themselves that everything is fine, know in their deepest selves that it is not. Their thoughts eventually manifest in their lives as obstacles: health problems, crime, betrayal by others, financial difficulties, infidelity, business failures, and more.

We pay a heavy price for our fear of failure. It is a powerful obstacle to growth. It assures the progressive narrowing of the personality and prevents exploration and experimentation. There is no learning without some difficulty and fumbling.

—John W. Gardner, *Self-Renewal*

THE PURPOSE OF FAILURE

But each obstacle in life has a purpose: to shock those deep in complacency and self-delusion back to reality. God's hope for all of us is that we will each discover our true power and destiny to order reality with the Divine Mind. But that does not come for those who think that manifestation means nothing more than ignoring the way things are and telling ourselves all is well when it is not. Obstacles and failures come into our orbit to remind us who we can be and mark the path for all we must do to evolve and grow into God's proxies. A wise older family member or friend has probably told you, whatever doesn't kill you makes you stronger. Like all such sayings, this one is simplistic in the real world, but it also has a kernel of solid truth.

THE LAW OF OBSTACLES

Failure and struggle are God's ways of waking us up to the need for enlightenment and giving us a path to evolve to our Divine potential.

Obstacles should not be cursed or avoided but welcomed as opportunities to grow and become more enlightened. None of us, even the most spiritually advanced, is immune to the blandishments of complacency, nor to the despair and anger that can wash over us when we attempt something that falls short and fails. But a realignment of our perceptions is in order. Obstacle and struggle awaken us to our wrong thinking and allow us to discover our true selves by stripping away falsehood and comfortable mediocrity. Failure is the greatest teacher in the cosmos. How often have you learned from something in which you succeeded? And how many times has failure led you to make changes that bred success in the future?

The key is not to become helpless or paralyzed in the face of obstacle and failure, such as a lost job. Psychologist Martin Seligman developed the concepts *learned optimism* and *learned helplessness* to identify the three most common attitudes held by those who perceive themselves as capable when faced with struggle and those who perceive themselves as helpless. You can imagine the power in this: helplessness is a choice, not destiny. You can teach the Divine Spirit in you to rise to the occasion rather than shrink from it.

In his research, Seligman identified three main qualities that defined "learned optimism" and "learned helplessness":

Learned Optimism

Impersonal—You see the cause of the failure as something outside your control. Sometimes, things happen.

Isolated—The failure does not affect all areas of life. Failure in one area says nothing about your ability to triumph in others.

Impermanent—The failure is temporary and in the future, and you know you can and will learn and do better.

Learned Helplessness

Personal—You decide you are responsible for what happened, no matter what caused the failure.

Pervasive—You see the failure as indicative of what happens in all areas of your life.

Permanent—You are resigned to the idea that you will never change and are condemned to this sort of failure again and again.[1]

It is easy to see how one attitude can be empowering while the other can be destructive. This mental perception of yourself shapes your ability to respond to obstacles and draw the potential blessings from their appearance.

---

1. Martin E. P. Seligman, *Learned Optimism: How to Change Your Mind and Your Life* (London: Vintage, 2006), http://www.shearonforschools.com/learned_optimism.htm.

Many scholars and laypersons alike have asked over the centuries, "Why would God allow struggle and hardship?" The answer is quite clear: because without them his children would have no means to grow and learn. Our very human tendency toward that empty version of manifestation rooted in denial and delusion makes us vulnerable to stagnation and spiritual rot. Only through confronting hardships and overcoming obstacles through work, discipline, self-belief, innovation, and faith do we truly come into our inheritance as children of God.

Failure and obstacles convey to us five critical lessons:

1. **Changing perception changes destiny.** What is the difference between a person who has spent years in complacent delusion and one who suddenly awakens to the reality that he or she must face struggles and risk failure to bring real change and wealth to life? Physically, nothing. But in the Mind and Spirit, where true reality lies, everything has changed. The path of each life is predictable in its meta nature: birth, growth, aging, and death leading to a passage to the next world. But within that cosmic framework, each individual life has the potential for infinite forms and convolutions. A change in thought—the true realization that we must abandon old patterns of thinking and face obstacles and that we have the Divine will to do so—abruptly reorders the path of any life into a new configuration.

   Instantly, the destiny of that person is transformed into something new and pregnant with spiritual potential. The adoption of the mind-set that we must accept hard times and break with the past in order to create a brighter future actually crystallizes that future into being the moment those thoughts take root. The caveat: the change must be lasting. We are all familiar with the outcome when someone feigns a true evolution in perception, which is actually just temporary: the alteration of the present and future is also temporary. Only by becoming that which you seek do you achieve it.

2. **Mental intention is continuous.** This lesson ties into the last. As I stated earlier, mental intention is always broadcasting into the Universe and bringing about results in our material lives. If we are troubled, those results are troubled—or violent or dysfunctional or ill. Yet as we can see when perception shifts and we become ready to face delusion and confront obstacles, intention instantly begins sending new waves of future manifestation into the ether. As long as the mind is alive, the power of the I Am is constant, always shaping destiny. The incredible effect of personal empowerment and facing obstacles reveals this to us. As soon as a person begins thinking more empowered thoughts, beneficial manifestations start taking shape.

3. **Obstacles indicate the opportunity for incoming good fortune.** Much of our trouble with times of struggle lies in our attitude toward them. We think of hard periods as times to be avoided, and we resent them as unwelcome visitors, when instead we should hail them as harbingers of good things to come. As thousands of successful entrepreneurs have said for centuries, failure is often the gateway to greater success and happiness. Obstacles themselves can both indicate a coming shift in fortune and serve as the catalyst for those new fortunes.

When you are cruising along in life at a moderate pace but afflicted with debt and a sense that you have missed your calling, it is not uncommon to camouflage the sadness and frustration of such a state with self-delusion. But then you lose your job and are thrust into a stage of life when self-reflection and departure from your comfortable mental life are inevitable. In this way, the obstacle of unemployment serves as the jumping-off point for changes in your perception and actions, but it also serves as the sign that if you seize the opportunity to reject delusion and evolve, far greater fortunes are coming.

It is an important step on the road to enlightenment to recognize and appreciate the importance and value of obstacles as signposts of our spiritual maturity—if we choose to follow them.

4. **Nothing "is." Things and people are always "becoming."** Permanence is an illusion. We exist in time, and because of this things and people are always in flux, always changing. Nothing is permanent in the physical world; only God and Spirit have permanence. Physical permanence is another human delusion that we maintain in order to give ourselves a sense of order in a chaotic universe. But the prevalence of obstacles and struggles proves to us that "is" is a mere mental construct. For what is the appearance of hardship in our lives but the appearance of sudden change, unbidden by us? A frightening diagnosis, a company closing, a sinking economy—these all represent change, nothing more. Whether we perceive them as blessings or curses depends on our perception. As Hamlet said, "Nothing is but that thinking makes it so."

Obstacles shatter our comforting illusion that anything can be static or lasting. Nothing is. But this is not cause for despair; that which does not change in this world stagnates and loses its relevance. Instead, we should embrace the changes that come and see them for what they are: reminders that nothing is certain but the love of God, and that we should cherish even the challenging periods in our lives, for they are chances to rise to unimagined heights.

5. **Obstacles are God's goldsmiths.** Each individual human being is like a bar of gold. We are beautiful, valuable, and most important, we are indestructible. Why is gold virtually impossible to destroy? Because it is malleable; that is, it can be transformed into virtually any shape—for coin, jewelry, architecture. This is why gold has been prized in every civilization and why items made of gold endure seemingly forever.

We have the same qualities. The reason that gold is so adaptable is that it is not hard and brittle like steel; it is soft and flexes with the stresses that come its way. We are the same when we are at our best. Obstacles and struggles are God's goldsmiths because they bring out in us those same qualities of adaptability and transformation. Every child of God possesses the ability to shape himself or herself into virtually any role, any life. We are without limit. Obstacles remind us of this and also evoke this quality in us. When we read of men or women who have endured years of trials and tribulations and losses only to rise again each time, we know we are witnessing lives of pure gold—lives we should strive to emulate.

▪   ▪   ▪   ▪   ▪

Gandhi said, "Freedom is not worth having if it does not include the freedom to make mistakes."[2] The freedom to face our own obstacles—and the freedom to choose whether we face them or try to avoid the opportunity they represent—is the essence of our role as children and proxies of God. We are always free so much as we can be within the bounds and rules of God's system, as we must be or we

---

2. http://thinkexist.com/quotation/freedom_is_not_worth_having_if_it_does_not/8068.html (accessed September 2009).

would be puppets, unable to learn or evolve. By being free to step over obstacles or be plowed under by them, we are liberated to become spiritual warriors for God's purpose.

THE LOSS OF A JOB OR CAREER SIGNALS A TIME OF SELF-REINVENTION

Some people will not choose to go this route, but given that 64 percent of Americans under twenty-five have said they are not satisfied with their jobs (a figure that is certain to rise as more people take jobs they don't like just to survive), more should.[3] The ending of an occupation is an opportunity to re-create your future by going in a new direction. You are freed from the pressure of performance but, at the same time, under the pressure of having to pay bills and find some means of support. In such a situation, the wise person will move toward re-creating an occupation for a simple reason: we always produce better results and greater satisfaction when we chart our own course.

The loss of a job or a break in a career brought about by a life change such as marriage or childbirth should be regarded not as a roadblock but a detour, an indicator that one's next move should be in another direction. It is a self-fulfilling prophecy of productive change that can propel any of us toward the occupation that brings us both greater meaning and closeness to God.

The block of granite which was an obstacle in the pathway of the weak becomes a stepping-stone in the pathway of the strong.
—Thomas Carlyle, "Theosophical Forum"

---

3. Associated Press, "Survey: More Americans Unhappy at Work," CBS News, January 5, 2010, http://www.cbsnews.com/stories/2010/01/05/national/main605661.shtml (accessed February 2010).

ECONOMIC HARDSHIPS
ENRICH US IN OTHER WAYS

The balancing forces of the cosmos mean that when a person encounters obstacles or struggles of a economic nature, the system of God is actively trying to enrich that individual in another aspect of the Divine economy. We saw this dynamic at work often as the recession played out: people who were rich in material wealth but poor in ethics, self-reflection, or compassion being forced by financial reversals to discover their talents in all those areas. In other words, they became wealthy in ways that would enhance their lives and move them toward completion as Divine beings, something that material wealth alone will not achieve.

We are a people who tend to focus primarily on material wealth. This is understandable; we live in a material world. Yet it is precisely our obsession with tangible wealth that can blind us to the very qualities that make that wealth possible. Obstacles force us to confront our shortcomings in the spiritual, mental, and emotional realms and, more important, to take steps to address them for our own well-being. By doing so, we enrich ourselves in myriad ways beyond the financial and, paradoxically, sow the seeds for many future great financial successes.

IF WE ENCOUNTER THE SAME OBSTACLES,
WE ARE NOT LEARNING

James Joyce said, "A man's errors are his portals of discovery."[4] In *The Bridge Across Forever*, author Richard Bach said, "There are no

---

4. http://thinkexist.com/quotation/a_mans_errors_are_his_portals_of_discovery/256217.htm (accessed October 2009).

mistakes. The events we bring upon ourselves, no matter how unpleasant, are necessary in order to learn what we need to learn; whatever steps we take, they're necessary to reach the places we've chosen to go." The message should be quite clear as expressed by these and other great thinkers: obstacles and errors are the world's teachers. If you encounter one obstacle and think that you have overcome it, only to encounter it again a few years later, then you did not surmount it at all. You deluded yourself into thinking that you became wiser, when all you did was dodge.

The purpose of obstacles, struggle, and failure is to help us learn and to become different people going forward—to shape a new destiny. If we do so, then we will continue to encounter obstacles, but because our minds and therefore our power to manifest outcomes and desires have changed, those obstacles will be different in kind and intensity. But if we do not transform who and what we are and only avoid the pain of change and confronting our failings, then we will be doomed to run against the same obstacles again and again—a kind of Sisyphean hell. For example, a man who endures the pain of a cheating spouse but who does not change his perception when choosing future mates will doubtlessly suffer the pain of infidelity again.

DETERMINATION IS OUR GREATEST ASSET

The great Alexander Hamilton, a founding father and the first treasurer of the United States, stated in *The Federalist Papers*, "There are strong minds in every walk of life that will rise superior to the disadvantages of situation, and will command the tribute due to their merit ..." Hamilton did not come from a privileged background as did many of his fellows. As related in this piece by Michael J. Gerson, he grew into a leader in part because he simply refused to be consigned to a future of poverty and meaninglessness:

Alexander Hamilton grew up in a family characterized by financial hardship, marital discord and bitter separations, public humiliations, parental death and abandonment. As a child, Alexander experienced ongoing tragedy, adversity and hardship. This early childhood environment serves as the unlikely backdrop for Alexander Hamilton's rise.

The story of Alexander Hamilton is a story of childhood deprivation and ongoing struggle. It is the story of a 10-year-old boy whose father leaves the family in a strange land with no money and an unemployed mother. It is the story of what happens when this boy's mother dies soon after, leaving 11-year-old Alex and his 13-year-old brother penniless, with an older cousin as a guardian. It is the story of how this 11-year-old boy reacts when, a year later, his cousin commits suicide, leaving him and his brother alone in the world with nothing other than their own emotional resources.

A resilient child is a term that psychologists give to children who seem to overcome multiple personal and family hardships, and survive despite great odds. And survive in the face of great odds is just what Alexander did. Given the experiences that Alexander encountered, we would predict that he would have had numerous difficulties of adjustment in later life. While he may well have struggled with his inner demons, the story of Alexander Hamilton is the story of a multiply challenged youngster who overcomes adverse personal and family circumstances to attain accomplishments of legend.[5]

---

5. Michael J. Gerson, "Adversity: The Childhood of Alexander Hamilton," *The Early American Review* Winter/Spring 2002, http://www.earlyamerica.com/review/2002_winter_spring/hamilton.html (accessed October 2009).

Simply refusing to give in and to continue striving to overcome a series of barriers and obstacles may be the greatest power we have as children of God. The will to survive and succeed is all-powerful.

WHAT WE HAVE LEARNED

- Complacency is the disease of self-delusion.

- Helplessness and power are based on how you perceive yourself.

- You are like gold: infinitely malleable. Obstacles are your goldsmiths.

- Determination and resilience rule the day.

14

THE LAW OF PARSIMONY

■ ■ ■ ■ ■

CORE PRINCIPLES

- You must spend your thought frugally.

- Choose the simplest possible course when reversing your fortunes.

- The more grasping your aims, the more unintended results you will attract.

As you simplify your life, the laws of the universe will be simpler; solitude will not be solitude, poverty will not be poverty, nor weakness weakness.

—Henry David Thoreau

*P*arsimony is a word with two meanings, both of them vital for our understanding of this Law of God. The first meaning of the word is "the state of being miserly or frugal." Certainly, given our economic times and the scarcity of income for many, this is a word whose time has come. To live parsimoniously is to survive when others are losing their means to house themselves, feed themselves, clothe themselves, and pay their debts. This meaning of parsimony has echoed down through the ages in great wisdom from thinkers like Da Vinci, Voltaire, and Plato. To save and to spend wisely and not wastefully has long been viewed as one of the great virtues of the evolved man. Yet the word has another, deeper meaning that dovetails elegantly with the first.

Parsimony also means a person chooses the simplest of all available choices. We often see the word in this context used when discussing causality and science. Those who refer to Occam's razor also talk about the need for parsimony: the tendency for the simplest possible explanation of a phenomenon to be the right one. Simplicity is universal. The cosmos seeks to conserve energy, so things are typically achieved in the simplest manner available.

Combining these two meanings under the Law of Parsimony forms a unique and powerful concept that can and should govern the intensity of our use of Divine Mind as well as our aspirations. Consider the individual who is faced with financial ruin. He grasps at any solution that presents itself and even when he has developed some awareness of the proper use of Divine Mind to manifest new prosperity, he often floods the ether with barely formed, undisciplined intention that he hopes will manifest something he wants. It is the gold panning approach to creating abundance—more is better, and if you wash a ton of rock, you may come away with an ounce of gold.

But more is not better. In fact, more can be damaging to your fortunes because, unlike the mountain stream that you know will always bring you more rock, the psychoreactive cosmos is not as predictable. As for simplicity, the panic response of the human mind when confronted with potential disaster compels us to reach for wild remedies to our problems. When a woman loses a job, she may not only employ her awareness of the I Am intention to manifest a new job into her life but in the desire to hedge her bets she may also try to manifest additional jobs, a new relationship, an inheritance, or some arcane scheme to bring wealth into her life.

God's system does not work in that way. The laws of the conservation of energy apply to spiritual energy, not just mechanical or electrical energy. When you project a desire into the spiritual realm and hold fast to that desire in your Divine Mind, the Universe usually brings that desire to fruition in the simplest way possible. Why? Because you must be able to handle what comes to you without it destroying who you are. We have discussed how so many lottery winners wind up bankrupt and in legal trouble. This is because they received abundance and complexity for which they were not prepared; their intention overrode the Divine system and granted them something that was a curse disguised as a blessing. This is the very definition of "be careful what you wish for."

The way to wealth depends on just two words, industry and frugality.
—Benjamin Franklin

THE TRUST OF SUFFICIENCY

Many, many individuals who violate this Law ignore frugality and instead spend copiously of their thought to try to bring into existence what they need. But why would this be an issue? Isn't the store of thought and wealth in the cosmos infinite? Isn't each human's store of intention infinite? Yes, but what is not infinite is the need of each person. For each of us, there is a finely calibrated level that guides what we need from the Universe to be happy, healthy, prosperous, and secure. We do not define that need; the system does. Beyond that level of need, we can acquire more and more if we adhere to a very simple but ironclad principle: *we must intend our excess abundance for the greater good.*

Very simply, a man may need only a solid job and a decent home to achieve his true wealth because that is the limit of his aspiration: a house, a loving relationship, wonderful children, and service to his community. If he works within God's system to manifest that need at that level, it will come to him quickly. If he decides that he wishes to exceed that level, he can do so but only if woven into this Divine Thought is the desire and intent to help others and enrich the world with what he attracts. The cosmos wants us to keep things simple, unless our goal is to create good for others. Then the bank vaults will open. But if our goals are selfish, then reckless spending of our mental capital leads to several possible consequences:

- The sabotage of the wealth we have already built.
- The exhaustion of our Mind's ability to focus on manifesting our goal.

- Unintended consequences coming into our material sphere.

There may be no greater example of the dangers of wealth not matching wisdom, and abundance exceeding need, than what has occurred on Wall Street. Wealth can corrupt. It does not corrupt all, but it corrupts many. Would it not be enough to acquire just what is needed now and gradually turn the gains into greater riches? Would it not be best to avoid the catastrophic collapse that we have seen, which comes with trying to amass more than we are prepared to handle? Parsimony is not about saving and not spending money. It is not about being cheap. No, it is about what we choose to buy with our thoughts. It is about having the enlightenment to spend our spirits wisely on the right things.

I cannot put this more simply than to say the Universe wants us to keep it simple and selfless. Look at the most successful impresarios in the world, from Sean Combs to Bill Gates. They have balanced their great wealth and power with great philanthropy, because they know that receiving great riches means giving great riches away. One is the seed of the other. When we give in to panic or greed and ask for the moon for selfish reasons alone, we often find the moon falling upon us.

THE LAW OF PARSIMONY

What you try to manifest with Mind for yourself alone should always be simple and frugal enough to meet your own needs and no more.

To the extent that you give, that is the extent to which you live. Lack of trust is born of fear. When we are in a position to lose our home, and we do not trust God's system to bring us the relief that we need at the level we need it, we react with panic. We hedge our bets by declaring our I Am not just to bring us a new job but an inheritance and a book contract and a lawsuit settlement. We don't trust that the cosmos will always bring us what we need to solve our problems while preserving our character. Parsimony comes when you can set aside your fear and believe that when you approach the system of God with the trust of sufficiency and the disciplined Mind that keeps the new fortune building in the spiritual realm, you will always find sufficiency.

WEALTH IS OUT THERE

All this is not to say that any of us should not desire financial abundance; that is a fundamental tenet of the prosperity gospel. However, many people misunderstand the meaning of that doctrine. There is no metric standard for meaningful wealth, no stage at which we can point to our bank account and say, "See, I have mastered God's system." Wealth means something different to everyone. One of the most irrefutable principles of the Universe is this: *for everything there is a price.*

The greater your wealth, the more you will pay in time away from family, physical exhaustion, hard work, or many other currencies. For some, a simple idea of wealth is something that gives them security while giving them the time, health, and peace to savor life. For them, that is prosperity. Others crave greater wealth but know that they must balance it with service and benefit to others. They are the billionaires, the captains of industry, the Oprah Winfreys and Sir Richard Bransons. They know that the way to mitigate the price of their great wealth on their heart and Minds is to give to others. They understand that not only is the service to something greater a precondition of the Universe manifesting wealth but the act of selfless service actually preserves the character qualities that enable them to maintain their wealth. I will go more into this idea in the chapter on the Law of Service.

So, parsimony is not intended to deny you the pursuit of abundance, but to temper it with wisdom. Do not fall prey to outside influences as to what or how much you should have; those who did that are now living in small apartments after losing their huge homes. We can see countless examples of this in our economy:

- States that have outspent their budgets and are now forced to cut services to children and the poor
- Companies undergoing massive, wrenching layoffs or going out of business completely
- Those formerly thought to be wealthy, who were actually deeply leveraged, now losing everything because they fell prey to "keeping up with the Joneses"
- Churches being forced to shut down or cancel expansion plans because they decided that growth was more important than service

It is very easy to become envious of what the "other guy" has and employ our great and Divine Minds in the pursuit of the petty and avaricious. But this only leads to the manifestation of things that can pull us aside from our character and ultimately lead us to loss and devastation. Notice in this economy that those people who were not seduced by easy home equity loans or creative investment ideas, who controlled their spending and invested wisely in their businesses, are doing okay. They are not doing cartwheels, but they are surviving and even thriving. This is the reward for understanding one's needs and listening to that inner voice rather than an outward trend. Some of us were born to be millionaires; others to lead simple, rewarding lives of love and service. There can be great nobility in both.

Ultimately, the cosmos will respond to the intention with which you saturate it; the system is impersonal and doesn't edit what it brings into our lives. We must indeed wish with care.

God is not a God of poverty nor of want. He is a God of abundance; money is that which does his bidding. He wants each of us to live in a fine mansion, wear fine clothes, travel to the finest places, and enjoy the best the material world has to offer. What many do not understand is that this idea is a metaphor for whatever each of us desires most. Many people do not wish to live in estates and drive Rolls-Royces; we relish a simple life of peace, devotion to others, and service to the Lord. Talk of mansions is really talk of the things that you desire most—relationships, health and vitality, purpose and passion, creativity and art, rich experiences ... as well as material security. However, too many of us are seduced by what we think we are supposed to want. This is the signpost on the road to ruin.

Parsimony reminds us that in simplicity of desire and frugality of thought lies the path to happiness. The truth is that as we grow in Mind and Spirit, the manifestation of our wealth will grow in concert with us. The simple desire of today is only of today; in five years, you may have grown into someone with deeper, more complex desires that reflect frugal thinking and true need but also bring you greater material abundance that you use to serve others along with yourself. We are never static; neither is what we manifest from God's system.

DESIRES GRANTED BY THE UNIVERSE

There seems to be a disconnect here, doesn't there? I have cautioned you that the Law of Parsimony frowns upon desires that are too complex to meet the innermost needs of the person who is trying to manifest them. Essentially, the manifestations of vanity. However, what if your true and meaningful desire is genuinely complex and requires a complicated chain of manifestation? Can the cosmos bring forth such a desire into your material experience?

The short answer is yes. There is no inherent prejudice against the complex and the arcane in God's system. It is just that the great majority of the time, such complex desires do reflect vanity and greed on the part of the person whose Mind is trained upon them, so results reflect those qualities. But if the need is true and there is an intention to enrich not just self but the community, then there is no reason why the forces of the cosmos cannot be marshaled to bring forth such results. Take, for example, a man who decides that his true calling is to create a children's theater company because he has a passion for the theater and feels the need to expose poor children in his community to it. Well, such an enterprise has many moving parts: a physical space, funding, actors, donors, equipment, and much more. That is a tall order. Yet if the man's desire is pure and strong, the Universe can indeed bring such manifestation forth.

Complexity is not the issue. The nature of the desire is. If it reflects something the person truly wants in the depths of his or her soul, complexity is no barrier to God's system.

Don't be Frugal in Your Wishes for Others' Good Fortune

An old saying suggests that "one can never be overgenerous with love nor too sparse with judgment." This is a sound idea behind the principle of parsimony: frugality of thought and wish does not apply when you are wishing good things for someone else. The norm is that:

1. The desire for someone else's good must be motivated by a pure desire for the other party's good, not by any hidden thought that you will ultimately benefit from that good fortune. Manifesting riches for someone else when you secretly harbor the hunger to turn that good fortune into your own is akin to doing an act of charity and then standing on the street corner announcing it to passersby: it empties the act of all meaning. There is no hiding our intent from the Universe; secret covetousness will produce the same poisoned fruit as overt covetousness.

2. The desire must be for someone worthy. There is nothing to be gained in trying to direct wealth toward someone who is violent, breaks the law, treats others badly, abuses drugs, or otherwise does ill in the world. There is nothing wrong with trying to help those who allow it, but since those who live destructively often turn new resources to the same destructive behavior, trying to manifest plenty in such lives will only wreak havoc.

Otherwise, be a spendthrift in your wishes for the good of others. In time, it will return to you multiplied many times over.

Save Intention for a Rainy Day

Frugality of thought and frugality of money share much in common, as they should: Mind is the currency of this world and should be spent with wisdom and discretion. But is it possible to save thought to use at another time, and is it desirable to do so? The answers are yes and yes. Not all thoughts and desires should be manifested at the time they seem fullest and ready for harvesting. This goes back to personal evolution: you may not be ready for something to manifest in your personal experience. It is extraordinarily difficult, when one has maintained the mental discipline to bring forth a desire into the physical world, to maintain that same discipline a second time, should that manifestation have proven to be more than you could handle the first time. Someone who wishes for her own business with all her heart, whether she has the maturity and experience to handle it, may find herself wishing that her desire had come to pass about ten years later if her company goes belly-up.

Once you develop the proficiency with Divine Mind to concentrate your I Am intention on manifesting what you most desire, it is both wise and good to marshal only the thoughts that suit where you are: the development of your emotions, skills, intellect, and knowledge of how to serve others. In other words, know thyself. The cosmos can be a harsh ecosystem for those who ask for that which they are not ready to manage. It is far better to tuck away ideas and visions for a time when you know they can reach their full and glorious fruition in you and fully benefit your entire community or even the world.

MAKE THE BEST OF COMPLEX MANIFESTATIONS

There are times when gifts given us out of pure love and compassion are too much to take. Someone could manifest something for you in your life that would prove to be more than your will or desires can tolerate, yet the person intended it as nothing more than a blessing upon you. Does this mean you are doomed to suffer the same pain as one who attracts something beyond his capacity into his own life?

Of course not. There is no cruelty in the cosmos. If the intention does not lie in your own Mind, then you will not suffer the hardships or enjoy the pleasures of good fortune that comes your way through another. You might briefly benefit, for example, from a monetary windfall that comes to you because of the mental intercession of someone else, but you will not acquire the knowledge or savvy to make that money return once it is spent. Of course, you will also not experience the upheaval and chaos that can come from such gifts. Your mind remains as it was before the windfall. So the best you can do is to do your best under such circumstances. Show gratitude for the intention, return what you can of the gift if you feel it has a corrupting quality, and try to learn what you can from the experience.

Unlimited abundance is not the purpose of the Universe. Unlimited potential for self-realization and inner riches is. We were not made and given the gift of Divine Mind in order to become rich for the sake of wealth; this was done so that we would become Creators in our own right and bring forth that which serves the purpose of God in the material world. The riches we are meant to bring forth are those that enrich us as Spirits and help us and others evolve into the beings of light that are our birthrights.

It is easy to lose sight of this reality. Our focus can so readily be turned to thoughts only of money and survival, and the lifeline of wealth for its own sake becomes very attractive. But know this: no hard times last forever. They always come to an end. What makes such periods in your life worthwhile and meaningful is that when the storm has passed, you are not the same. You have evolved! You have become a being closer to God's ideal and more capable of wielding the wealth of bank account, Mind, and Spirit to do his bidding and work his will. That is the ultimate goal of any hardship. The wealth that the cosmos brings us is only about money, homes, cars, and power on the surface. Beneath, it is about using those things to bring about positive change in ourselves and the world around us. The discipline and wisdom wrought by the Law of Parsimony are vital in order that you become the being that God invented his system to help you become.

WHAT WE HAVE LEARNED

- Frugality of mind prevents the waste of your thoughts when you are not ready for their consequences.

- You must trust that God's system will bring you no more or less than what you need or can manage at the time.

- The definition of true wealth is different for each of us.

- Money is not the ultimate goal; growth into a higher being is.

15

THE LAW OF
QUANTUM ABUNDANCE

⬛ ⬛ ⬛ ⬛ ⬛

CORE PRINCIPLES

- The Universe is a quantum system built on Consciousness.

- All possibilities exist until they are perceived by the living Mind.

- All opportunities exist for you in the realm of the Mind, waiting to crystallize.

Quantum theory also tells us that the world is not simply objective; somehow it's something more subtle than that. In some sense it is veiled from us, but it has a structure that we can understand.

—John Polkinghorne[1]

Quantum mechanics has been burdened in recent years with the pejorative *pseudoscience*, largely because it has been used as a catchall to lend credibility to virtually any New Age product, theory, or treatment. But set all that aside and realize that quantum theory is the single most successful theory in the history of science. Not one of its predictions has ever been disproved. And as much as materialistic scientists wish this were not the case, quantum mechanics, or QM, reveals that the universe is fundamentally based on Consciousness. This goes against much prevailing wisdom that says that the cosmos is a purely mechanistic environment devoid of free will, purpose, or Deity, so many simply cannot cope with the reality of QM's central role. But more and more experiments are revealing to science what we have known in the spiritual disciplines for many generations: existence is built on Mind.

This has vast and exciting implications for personal enlightenment and the manifestation of wealth and abundance, especially in the difficult economic times we face. For countless years, ever since

---

1. Lyndon F. Harris, "Divine Action: An Interview with John Polkinghorne," *Cross Currents*, 48 (1), 1998.

the age ironically known as the Enlightenment of the mid-nineteenth century, when science began to displace religion as the dominant explanatory force in life, people have explained wealth in the same way they explained humanity. According to the purely materialistic view, we are nothing more than packs of neurons with no free will, no real minds, and no spirit. We are wet computers that live and die meaninglessly and whose only purpose is to pass on our DNA. In the same way, this bleak and empty philosophy has been applied to money. Money, the sophists claim, is just currency roaming around in computers. It is dead, static, and finite.

Quantum physics thus reveals a basic oneness of the universe.
—**Erwin Schrödinger, "On Truth and Reality"**

Just as we know this eliminative view of humanity to be false, we can see that the same perspective on money is equally spurious. Wealth is immaterial; it is God's power of change made manifest in the world. It is limitless. And it is an active, evolving force in the world, a form of potential energy that transforms into kinetic energy when a person applies it to create or build something. Money and abundance are based on the quantum reality that underlies all things, so your own opportunities to create your future of financial security are without limit. You are not condemned to choose between one meager possibility or another, bound by a poor economy and shattered finances. Instead, the quantum nature of wealth means that you can literally sift through all possibilities that you have ever imagined for your life and choose from them all, like a woman selecting earrings from an overflowing jewel box. QM dictates that all possibilities that have ever manifested in Mind also must take form in material reality at some point in the past, present, or future. So you can in fact create your own future in whatever form you wish.

There are, of course, limits to this that are self-imposed. Scenarios that are greedy or harmful will almost always backfire on the person doing the manifesting. The more complicated and rich the desired outcome, the greater the mental discipline needed to manifest it. And if your character, wisdom, and judgment are not prepared to properly use what God's system brings you, then you can experience severe consequences. These limits are necessary because of the truly limitless power of quantum Mind. We cannot all be kings of the world. We are called to evolve and grow in compassion and self-perception.

However, you are free to transcend the apparent limits of economics for a broader universal economic reality: the currency of thought. Abundance exists as a basic state of the cosmos; scarcity is something created by humans and our limited minds. So by using the power of thought to tap into that abundance and bring it into material coherence, you can achieve any state of wealth or security to which you set your Mind.

THE LAW OF QUANTUM ABUNDANCE

All possibilities for your wealth and enrichment exist all around you as quantum potentials. By locking your attention on a possibility, you collapse it into a reality and bring about that abundance.

The hyphothesizing of quantum theory back in the early twentieth century rocked the world of science and physics. Even the great Einstein was so unnerved by the potential effects of this system of explaining reality on the subatomic level that he did everything he could to disprove it, without success. The implications of QM—the oneness of all things and beings, the creation of material reality by the observation of Mind—are world shifting for science and for our society as a whole. Imagine what would come about if the world grasped the noetic truth that all people are one? It would revolutionize this global culture.

However, the ignorance of the broader populace does not condemn us to reside in a disconnected, mechanistic cosmos. Quite the contrary; we can do much in using the reality of quantum abundance to improve our lives and the lives of those around us. But first, we must understand what a quantum underpinning to the universe means and does not mean. The essential idea to remember about quantum reality is this: in the universe, all potentialities and possibilities exist, suspended in a state of indeterminacy. That is the ether of Spirit, God's workshop. When a Mind locks onto a possibility, the energy of that Mind's attention instantly transforms that probability into a reality. This applies to elementary particles like electrons and photons and also to situations in life. This is what gives us all the power to manifest new destinies and new abundance with our directed mental intention.

Beyond this, there are four new and empowering realities that spring from quantum abundance that you must know:

1. **You are not locked into destiny.** Some claim that the universe is purely deterministic—that is, God has set the cosmic gears in motion, and we are completely helpless to alter our progression through the course of time. Natural laws determine everything we can and will do. This is patently nonsense. Instead, QM gives us the freedom to choose our futures. Nothing is set in stone; nothing is certain for good or ill.

   Take the story of Liz Murray as an example of this. Raised by a drug-addicted mother, she ended up as a homeless teen on the streets, and then sobbing on the top of her mother's bare pine casket as she realized she was headed for the same fate as her mother—a premature, lonely death—unless she changed something. So she did. She decided that she would attend Harvard University. Now, this was an audacious goal, a young girl with no address getting into the most prestigious university in the nation. Yet Liz fixed her will and intention on this goal and did not let up. Four years later, she made it into Harvard. She had defied what could have been her destiny with the might of her Mind and transformed her future.[2]

This should be an instructive lesson for all of us who have more than Liz but perhaps aspire to less. We are not meant to do anything except be fulfilled and complete in God's service. We are not trapped by anything but our own perceptions of our limitations.

2. **Everything is possible until Mind decides.** If you don't believe that literally anything can happen, talk to someone who has been struck by lightning five times. Talk to Jim Cole, a naturalist who has been mauled not once but twice by grizzly bears and lived to tell the tale. Talk to anyone who has received a shocking windfall or reconnected with a lost friend or love on a city street after not being in contact for forty years. Because all possibilities in the cosmos are frozen in suspension due to quantum mechanics, there is the potential that anything, no matter how far-fetched, can occur. This accounts for natural disasters and stock market collapses, but also for miraculous healings and incredible coincidences.

This means that anything is possible for you, too. You need not resign yourself to something; new realities can bloom into your future in a matter of seconds. As the Bible states, you know

---

2. Liz Murray, *Breaking Night: A Memoir of Forgiveness, Survival, and My Journey from Homeless to Harvard* (New York: Hyperion, 2010).

neither the day nor the hour. What that refers to is that miraculous events can transpire in your experience at any time. More important, no matter what your great desire is and no matter how remote it might seem, it is just as possible as you walking across the street. In the eyes of the universe, there is no difference in the probability of you launching a software company and having a net worth equal to Bill Gates's and the probability of you yawning when you wake up in the morning. It is all a matter of mental and intentional focus and discipline.

3. **Money collapses thought into action.** Money actually exists in a quantum state of duality: material in outward manifestation, yet its true potential exists as an idea, a mental state. But what people do not realize about money is that because it is essentially a state of quantum consciousness, it has the power to collapse probability into dynamic action. Money serves the quantum reality of the cosmos. Think about what happens when an entrepreneur has an idea. The idea exists as potential energy until money is applied to it. Then it comes into being as concrete action and forward motion. This is the true meaning and power of money: not to buy products but to unfold ideas from probability into working existence and evolution.

In essence, money is an evolutionary force that sets the realized possibility of the Mind into forward motion, into becoming and changing. It is the next stage in the process of manifestation. First, possibilities exist in infinite quantity but zero certainty. Then, mental intention crystallizes a single potential into reality in Mind. Finally, as the mental reality enters our awareness as an idea, money takes that idea from the incorporeal to the corporeal, setting energies in motion to produce new things, new meanings, new organizations, and new ways of being.

Money is quantum energy made material. It is the power to exert will over randomness. Keep this in mind when you think about what you will do with your money and you will not take it lightly.

4. **Your financial situation is a reflection of your thought.** This is a hard pill for some to swallow. No one wants to believe that her debt, her foreclosure, or her poverty is a result of her mental state, but it is. Nothing manipulates the stuff of potential and reality but thought, so all things are caused by mental energies. More to the point, our habitual thoughts and our actions (which are driven by thought) craft our destinies. So your financial situation is a product of how your habitual thoughts of money and wealth have shaped the manifestation energies flowing toward your corporeal experience.

This is why the prosperity gospel makes a point of saying that you must think and act as though you are wealthy, because actions spring from thoughts and your thoughts turn possibility into formed actuality. If you focus your Mind on poverty and want, then your mighty thoughts will reach into the quantum substrate of unformed possibilities and attract to you those that translate into more want and poverty. Like calls to like. So you can have a man who has worked hard all his life and done nothing wrong in terms of overspending or buying a house that was too big for his budget, but who loses his home anyway. Because his focus is always on the lack of funds and what he and his family do not have, this negative and defeating thought pattern collapses similar potential into his life in the form of job loss, costly needed medical care, or some other event that destroys his family's finances.

It is not fair, but it is reality. Dwell on greed and the quantum reality will bring greed into your life as those who covet what you have. Dwell on riches even when you are barely getting by and the cosmos will reward that habitual thought with opportunity, security, and abundance.

❚❚   ❚❚   ❚❚   ❚❚   ❚❚

The most important thing about the quantum nature of reality is that it robs us of any last hope of passivity in the determination of our fate. The fatalistic religiosity of old must give way to a more active, self-starting form of spirituality that recognizes that God is not the prime mover in our destiny. We are. God created the framework in which we carry out our lives, but what occurs within that framework is up to our choice and our mental discipline. However, far too many men and women fail to understand this and stand around idly waiting for God to grant their wishes for wealth and new opportunity. This leads to greater poverty and frustration, lost opportunity to improve the lives of many as people fail to realize their potential due to inaction.

It is my hope that this information can serve as the beginning of an awakening to the reality of God as system and principle, not puppet master or fairy godfather. We are the captains of our souls, and quantum abundance points the way to how we can use our Minds to transform our futures.

This is one of the strongest bones of contention among those who encounter the implications of the quantum universe. The idea that someone could bring on his or her own financial ruin is deeply offensive to many, but that idea is a misunderstanding of the nature of Divine Mind. To "deserve" one's fate, one must also produce that fate with intention. A man who approaches others with a spirit of envy, covetousness, or anger that leads to negative actions reaps precisely what he deserves. That is a deserved fate because the actions had harmful intent behind them.

However, thoughts of envy or rage or poverty that do not lead to actions, but instead are born of an ignorance of the Laws of Prosperity and the psychoreactive nature of the cosmos, have no intent behind them. A man who dwells on his poverty but otherwise merely works hard does not intend to bring down misfortune on himself, but he sometimes does. This is the price of ignorance of the nature of reality, in much the same way that a person who is ignorant of a law can nonetheless be prosecuted and jailed for its violation. Maintaining harmful mental patterns can bring down trouble on one's head, but it is not deserved. It is not a judgment on one's fitness, worth, or holiness. It is a painful illustration of the perils of not understanding how God's universe operates.

Doing is a quantum leap from imagining.
—Barbara Sher, *I Could Do Anything If I Only Knew What It Was*

THE UNCERTAINTY PRINCIPLE

The Heisenberg uncertainty principle is at the heart of quantum mechanics and the quantum nature of our lives. It says that while we can know one aspect of the nature of a particle of matter, we can never know all of them at the same time. So there is an inherent quality of unpredictability to all of nature. We do not have the power to know what will happen no matter how well we prepare or how obsessively we work to control things. Only God has the power to transcend the physical laws of nature by operating purely in spirit.

This means that despite our best efforts and our organization, planning, and work, we cannot know what will come of our intention. Part of an intention may manifest while another does not; an intention may manifest but in a different form from what we have in mind. The result of the intention coming to pass may produce consequences far different from what we desired, for better or worse. There is simply no way to control what comes to pass. If intention is pure and strong, you can count on much of a worthy intention coming to fruition, but the basic uncertainty of manifestation is a fundamental aspect of the universe.

This is not bad news. It is quite freeing. It frees us from having to try to exercise control over every aspect of what we try to create in our material experiences. We cannot, so we do not need to worry or feel anxiety over what might happen. Since control is an illusion, quantum abundance liberates us to focus on the things we can control—our Mind, discipline, wisdom, and integrity—and let go of worry about things we cannot control. Thus, uncertainty lends greater joy and peace to life because it absolves us of some of the responsibilities we heap on our own shoulders.

PROPHETS CAN HELP YOU OVERCOME UNCERTAINTY

Prophecy offers a single loophole in the essential uncertainty of mental manifestation because genuine prophets are directly in touch with the Mind of God and thus partially working with senses that lie beyond the limitations of physical laws. While prophecy cannot master the unpredictability of the cosmos, it can mitigate it in some cases. The prophet provides guidance that can aid the seeker in making decisions or taking actions that can either prevent misfortune or promote good fortune. Provided this guidance is heeded, the inborn randomness of reality can be dampened.

A prophet is one who is trained in the discipline of Mind that channels the awareness of God, which transcends space and time, into a human vessel. Experienced and gifted prophets can be great assets to others. Yet prophecy is not a guarantee. Even the greatest prophet can neither predict all events nor deliver guidance with perfect accuracy. The portents and currents of the cosmos are subtle and unpredictable at the best of times, and they cannot always easily be mastered. But if you are attempting to become more enlightened and turn the quantum reality of existence into a benefit for your future, a link with a prophetic individual can be a great boon.

THE QUANTUM REALITY MEANS WEALTH IS ENTANGLED

Earlier, we discussed the Law of Entanglement, in which all things are one. Entanglement is a quantum phenomenon and because of this, wealth for one is the potential for wealth for all. Wealth, abundance, health, security—all the states that we desire—are contagious, in a way. Because all Minds remain entangled, when you manifest wealth and good financial fortune for yourself, you are subtly pushing those in your orbit toward the same result. When you dwell on poverty or try to manifest a result motivated by greed or envy, you also nudge the energies of those around you in that same downward direction. Good fortune and misfortune become embedded in the mental ecosystem of your family, friends, colleagues, and others who know you. It is because of this that a person who maintains a powerful spiritual mind-set often breeds power and benefit for many.

This means that your responsibility for comprehending and making proper use of the immense power of Divine Mind is not only for your own future but for those about whom you care. You affect their manifestations as they affect yours. This could be called the "rising tide lifts all boats" effect of Mind: as one goes, so go all. Of course, mighty mental discipline and attention can overcome the currents of those people who might influence you, but many people do not have such strength of mind. It pays then not only to master your own manifestation but to help enlighten those in your community so they can guide your communal results toward greater abundance, wealth, joy, and health.

This law represents the perfect blend of science and spirituality, which are, after all, two sides of the same coin of discovery. Both reveal, in different contexts, that we inhabit a universe of Mind where possibilities are limitless and personal responsibility for our own destiny is paramount. Because anything that you could wish for exists in stasis in the spiritual plane, it is possible to achieve your dreams by dreaming them while walking in the waking world. Focus attention on the impossible, and it becomes possible. In this way do we transform the world, shape the future beyond our own lives, and bring greater healing and hope to others.

WHAT WE HAVE LEARNED

- Quantum mechanics means all possibilities can come to pass.

- You cannot control all things, so you are free to worry about only that which we can control.

- Prophets can overcome some of the inherent unpredictability of the cosmos.

- Entanglement means your manifestations and intentions affect those of others.

16

THE LAW OF RECESSION

■ ■ ■ ■ ■

CORE PRINCIPLES

- All material and spiritual fortune runs in cycles.

- There will always be times when wealth recedes from your life.

- Recession occurs to prepare you for the next cycle.

The greater the emphasis on perfection, the further it recedes.
—Haridas Chaudhuri, Bengali philosopher

In this new century we live in, the word *recession* is more often than not viewed as profanity, at least when it is not taking the place of our ancient concept of the devil. Deep in debt? Blame the recession. Depressed and feeling hopeless about the future? It's the recession's fault. In danger of losing your home? It must be the recession, not the dangerous adjustable-rate mortgage you got. The recession has become our catchall for all the ills that flesh is heir to. Yet most people fail to understand what a recession truly is. It is merely the natural and inevitable trough that follows in the progression of cycles that affect all of human activity. As we have discussed before, all things in the cosmos must fall in balance, from human life and death to economic activity. The reason for this is that the purpose of the material universe is for conscious beings to evolve toward greater and greater spiritual potential, and this would not occur in a static state. If you existed either in a state of constant wealth and abundance or in one of constant poverty and despair, you would neither change nor grow. God has a vested interest in the development of every spirit into which he has poured himself. Therefore, we live in a universe of ever-shifting balances.

We see this in the age-old concept of yin and yang: hot and cold, movement and stillness, love and hatred. We see it in the opposites that are an inherent part of religious teaching: love thy enemy, when you want more of something give it away, and so on. In our economic lives, balance is everywhere and constantly adjusting. The word *recession* means "to pull away," as when the waters of a flood recede from the devastated area. In economic terms, we confuse recession with some sort of similar destruction, but that is merely a misunderstanding of the reality of God's economic system. Recession is simply the balance reshifting back toward the center after a period during which it was artificially shifted to the opposite extreme. When recession occurs, fortunes become reversed. The rich become poor. The meek inherit more of the earth, if not all of it. Chaos replaces order. It is the sermon on the mount come to pass in God's Kingdom—which is, after all, not some mythical heaven but his economic system right here on earth.

The trouble is that when we exist in an unenlightened state, we are subject to the same limits on perception as are all people: namely, we are trapped in present panic rather than free to see future hope. Think of the emotions that may have accompanied your own economic troubles, from job layoffs to the loss of home equity to perhaps a bankruptcy or frightening medical bills: fear, worry, anger, desperation, confusion. All these feelings serve to blind us to the larger perspective that this is all part of a natural cycle brought about by unnatural economic conditions set forth by the hand of humankind in violation of God's laws.

The cosmos is not a place of extremes. Yes, there are extreme events, from stock market collapses and wars to tsunamis and epidemics, but they are temporary. By and large, the small bumps in the progression of reality quickly recede, and we return to a modicum of balance, with some wealth, some poverty, some war, some peace, and a great deal in between. In this ecosystem of the Spirit, we strive and work and slowly progress in our personal evolution. But when forces hold the extreme state in place, energies build up that cannot be sustained. The global economy was held in an extreme state, like the thirty-foot wave of a tsunami is held in place as it is about to crash on shore, by arcane financial tools, speculation, and consumer debt. But one cannot hold a titanic force like a wave or an economy in an extreme state for long, because the forces needed to do so are monstrous and impossible to maintain. When the extreme state finally bursts, the results are apocalyptic. With the wave, communities are wiped off the face of the earth. With the economy, livelihoods suffer the same fate.

Recession exists to prevent this type of shattering defiance of the natural balance. It pulls us back toward the center when conditions in the material realm tip too far to one side. It is the natural cycle of things returning to the way they are supposed to be. There should not be too much easy wealth based on speculation and greed. There should not be industrial activity that enriches a few while impoverishing the environment. There should not be spending that fuels exploitation and slavery in the labor markets of poor countries. There should not be such wealth that we spend all our time serving ourselves and not each other. Recession is a tool of should.

THE LAW OF RECESSION

The forces of the cosmos will withdraw wealth and prosperity in some measure when society falls too far out of balance in order to create conditions under which we may evolve, grow, and serve each other.

Recession can be a terrifying idea for many of us. After all, our material prosperity is the means by which we create our lives and affect the community around us. The poor do not create change. The poor have no power. They are dependent on others for their very lives. That impotence frightens and paralyzes, so we do whatever we can to avoid it. But it is not necessary to fear recession, if you understand it. Remember, it is only the natural cycle of things reasserting itself after a period of gross imbalance. Painful as the temporary results may be, in the long-term recession restores the health of our spiritual ecosystem.

For your own personal prosperity, however, the idea of recession seems to promise disaster, but this need not be the case. There are two critical principles of recession that we will analyze in this chapter, and the first is this: *the greater the imbalance, the more shocking and severe the swing back to the center.*

We have seen this with the global economy. Years of recklessness have led to catastrophic job loss, government service cuts, the loss of millions of homes and trillions in retirement savings ... The list of woes goes on. This dive into a canyon of pain was brought about precisely because we climbed so high on a mountain of false prosperity built on leveraging and illusory value. The higher we rise, the farther we have to fall—if we rise too quickly or if our rise is based on factors other than our own spiritual strength, personal character, and service to others.

There are dilettantes who spend fortunes to climb Mount Everest, hiring others to carry all their gear for them and guide them to make up for their lack of mountaineering experience and physical fitness. Yes, they can possibly ascend high on the mountain, but what happens if disaster strikes? Answer: they are less equipped to survive than others who may have paid more of a price being prepared to climb the mountain and who are strong enough to make it down should a storm occur.

Think of those people you know who have weathered a recession with relatively little trouble. They are almost always those who did not act rashly when times were booming. They did not borrow against their homes multiple times. They did not spend recklessly. They maintained as much fiscal balance in their own lives as they possibly could. They were conservative. By not getting too high on the mountain, they did not have far to fall. When the cycle is balanced, they will be the ones in the best position to grow once again.

In order to avoid financial ruin in your own life, you must practice the same kind of self-discipline and wisdom. Maintain balance even when the situation outside your doors is becoming unbalanced. Be aware of the cycle and that the higher you fly, the further you can fall. I am not counseling you to take a vow of poverty or settle for the middle class when you have wealth inherent in your Divine Mind. No! However, I am suggesting that in trying to manifest your own prosperity and create your wealth, you take the slow, careful course that is lined with spiritual maturity, character, and the goal of service to others. This is the path to great wealth tempered with balance. Otherwise, you can become like the ship captain who maneuvers toward his goal so quickly that his cargo shifts suddenly and capsizes the vessel. Gradual, careful, prudent movement toward abundance and greatness is virtually recession-proof.

Each thing is of like form from everlasting and comes round again in its cycle.

—**Marcus Aurelius,** *Meditations ii14*

IN THE SHIFTING BALANCE IS OPPORTUNITY

The second core truth about recession is that there is a consistent amount of wealth in the cosmos existing as the potential of change.

That means that a recession does not destroy prosperity, because it cannot be destroyed. Recession simply shifts the realized energy of material wealth back into the potential energy of manifestation, making it available for others to manifest. So when you witness a recession, remember that in the shifting balance of wealth from material to mental, potential energy is vast opportunity for you to create your own prosperous future.

This is borne out in our world as it is progressing today through its financial dire straits. Despite the job losses and fiscal disaster, there are those making money, starting businesses, and prospering. The potential energy of wealth exists everywhere: in undervalued real estate, in new company ideas that serve aspects of the transformed economy brought about by the recession, in wise investing, in education, and in countless other sectors of human activity. Healthcare careers are thriving during these dark times. So is personal coaching. Consultants who can help companies and individuals reinvent themselves for the new future are doing well. Those with the ability to understand the dynamic of the shifting balance and identify ways in which new opportunity is blossoming are becoming wealthy.

You can do the same thing on a large or small scale. With the awareness of this dynamic operating all around you, you can see where God's system is working to reassert the balance and take advantage. Look around and you will see aspects of the material economy where the waters are receding and leaving the debris that can be built into a new future. For example, the real estate market has of course been savaged, but in that wreckage lie new opportunities: investments, rental properties, and so on. The saying "it is an ill wind that blows no one any good" is very true in our modern world. Build a windmill.

This is not to say, of course, that you should exploit the misfortune of others. That is precisely the kind of activity that brings about the extreme shifts in fortunes that lead to destruction. Know this: there are recessions in God's system, and there are recessions in your own personal economy. Sometimes the two are linked; sometimes they act independently. It is possible to thrive while all those around you are suffering, and to suffer while they are thriving. Your best defense is maintenance of your personal balance built on discretion, mental discipline, love, and service. If you try to leverage the losses of others, you will manifest greed by harboring such thoughts.

Recession is yet another reminder that the state of the universe is one of change—of becoming, not being. All things fall into cycles, from the seasons to human lives. To know these seasons and cycles and respect them for what they are allows us both to take preventive, foresighted action to avoid disaster and to make the most of opportunities that arise when the new cycle begins. As with all things, it is an understanding of the mechanisms by which God governs the cosmos that empowers us, even though we did not create the laws by which he governs. Any system has its inherent advantages and disadvantages, strengths and weaknesses.

As we have seen with the current economic situation, "crisis" is a matter of perspective and degree. For those who react with panic and desperate action, the outset of the next recessive cycle may indeed be a tsunami of hardship and pain. For those enlightened ones who understand the nature of events and see the big picture, the crisis can instead be a time of growth, of positive change and the securing of an improved position in life. Before each of us lies the choice of which of those paths to take.

THE CYCLE OF RECESSION FOLLOWS A PREDICTABLE PATTERN

Each cyclical period of recession obeys a Divine template as it unfolds. First, there are warning signs that a period of great prosperity or ease of generating wealth is not only coming to an end, but may have been buoyed by false conditions. Then there is a tipping point, in which one vital support for the way things were suddenly collapses (witness the fall of Lehman Brothers investment bank). Following this, there is an extended time of pulling away when things that were once easy, such as generating business, become torturous and difficult, if not impossible. After this comes a time of despair, a "wailing and gnashing of teeth" period when those who are not enlightened panic.

Meanwhile, those who enjoy a deeper perception begin to survey the landscape for opportunities. The next stage comes when those opportunities begin to appear and take root. Finally, the new opportunities, plus a clearing of the deadwood from the old situation, causes the recession to "bottom out" and growth begins anew. This is the eternal cycle, and while the severity of the cyclical peaks and troughs varies, the cycles will never end. They are a part of God's system and a part of human evolution. Knowing this pattern, however, is a key to mastering the cycles and riding these waves instead of being plowed under by them.

A RECESSION CAN OCCUR IN ANY AREA OF YOUR LIFE

Recessions do not just occur in financial and economic systems. The principle of recession is the pulling back of opportunity and ease in order to correct a prior cycle of overabundance and ease that put things out of balance. Remember, we exist as proxies for God in order to allow him to evolve, and the material plane is our crucible where we are tested and driven closer and closer to perfection by hardship and striving and entrepreneurship. Eventually, we leave this life and return to God as pure Spirit, bringing with us that essence of Mind that we have honed and evolved and adding it to the Divine whole. In the unimaginable span of future time, we will one day complete the evolution of God and our purpose will have ended, though no one can know when this will come to pass.

So within the ecosystem of the physical, the cycles of struggle and triumph are constantly playing out in all areas of human life. Recession is universal and asynchronous—one aspect of your life can be in a cycle of riotous growth and ease while another can be in recession. In fact, most human lives follow this pattern. It is not uncommon to see a person who, while his career is thriving and money comes easily, is in recession in his relationships, his marriage breaking down, his children becoming distant and sullen. Similarly, some people experience personal financial recession while at the same time undergoing tremendous expansion in spiritual life and faith.

Knowing this, you will gain a greater understanding of the seasons of your own life and a comprehension of why they occur. Just as entrepreneurs look for opportunities in the rubble of a fallen economy, you can find hope and new chances for growth, self-reinvention, and positive transformation even in your darkest hours. Witness those who change their lives after cancer or discover a joyous new career after a layoff. They are harbingers of hope.

RECESSION IS ALWAYS FOLLOWED BY A PERIOD OF EXPANSION

This is the hope that many people hold out for during a period of recession: the bounce that inevitably comes after the weakness and corruption are purged from the economic system. Since the world and the energies of human life run in cycles, it is inevitable that the descent of recession will be followed by expansion. However, recovering from a recessive period in your life, whether it is a larger economic collapse or a personal pullback in your health, relationships, or career, is not simply a matter of hunkering down and waiting until things go back to the way they used to be. No, for recession to become expansion in the spiritual sense, there must be change.

For expansion to follow contraction in your own experience, you must use the period of recession to spark an expansion of your Divine Mind and your self. This means that you must use the obstacles and violent change of a down period to grow: to discover new mental discipline in your I Am intention, to find ways to serve others, to shed negative relationships, to discover a closer meditative connection to the Mind of God. In short, you must expand before your personal economy will expand. You must become the growth you wish to see in your own fortunes. If you do not, then yes, economic conditions will turn around at some point, but you will merely reenter that environment with the same weaknesses that drove your fortunes down in the previous cycle. Your own spiritual and mental expansion plants the seed for your coming economic expansion.

THE PERSONAL STIMULUS PACKAGE

The idea of economic stimulus has been put into action in order to stem the flow of recession. This can work, but as with the larger economy, the effectiveness of stimulus depends on its precision. In the case of our personal spiritual development, risk is a "stimulus package" that will prompt the kind of growth that sparks new opportunity and expansion. God wants us each to step out on the edge with only Him as our means of spiritual, mental, and financial support. When we do, that risk sparks astonishing change.

Do not always be afraid of what some may consider dangerous. When recession comes, instead of following the burrowing instinct held to by so many, go the opposite way. Look into your heart and find that risk that thrills you and serves the purpose placed in your spirit by God, and follow it. Do what is dangerous, what makes you uncomfortable, what appears foolish to others. In foolishness lies wisdom. This might mean quitting your job to pursue a different career, moving to a new location, trying a physical risk that previously frightened you, or starting your own company. Risk redirects the energies of manifestation in our lives by changing our thoughts—intensifying them by the stimulation of the new. As we discover new capabilities and passions, we reshape our intentions and the results that manifest. This stimulus effect brings new people, opportunities, discoveries, creative thoughts and abundance into our spheres of consciousness.

> *Spiritual and religious traditions ... affirm the cyclical phases of our lives and the wisdom each phase brings, the sacredness of our bodies and the body of the Earth.*
>
> —Patrice Wynne

Stimulus is not a guarantee of future prosperity, but it is a mechanism designed to put that prosperity into place eventually. In the vastness of time, when you stimulate sectors of your personal economy with new energies, you break your old paradigms. You set aside the past and engage in deliberate evolution of Body, Mind, and Spirit. The results will always take you beyond the limited panic and desperation of the recessive cycle and into a new future of self-awareness and empowerment.

Since recession so often revolves around economics, and money represents God's power of change in our lives, the recessive force will most often play out in our financial spheres. With money being such a source of emotion, emotional equanimity is the most important skill to develop as you work to recognize and leverage the recessive cycles in your life. Frantic action is useless action. It is the herd mentality at work, being a sheep instead of a shepherd. Instead, cultivate calm and detachment from the economic conditions of your life by seeing them as what they truly are: mileposts on the road to your personal evolution. Nothing more.

Perspective is everything. As you grow in your perspective of God's Laws and his system, you will begin to reflexively see times of recession not as cause for alarm but as times to give more to your church, do more for others, leap into the void with a new business— in short, do exactly the opposite of what is expected. That is faith in the future. In fact, the future is the opposite of today. Recession reverses course and becomes expansion. Sickness becomes health. Barrenness becomes fertility. Dark becomes light. You exist in a realm of cyclical opposites, and by defying convention and engaging in those opposites, you engage the future. You create the future.

WHAT WE HAVE LEARNED

- Recession is the cyclical act of natural balance reasserting itself.

- The greater the false height, the faster the fall into recession.

- Panic and emotionality thwart personal evolution.

- You must risk and engage in behavior that is the opposite of what you normally do in order to transform your fortunes from recession to expansion.

17

THE LAW OF RISING TIDE

■ ■ ■ ■ ■

CORE PRINCIPLES

- The world's economic currents are complex and too subtle for anyone to comprehend.

- In many ways, what benefits others will also benefit you.

- Therefore, rejoice in the good fortunes of others rather than regarding them with envy.

There is a tide in the affairs of men, which taken at the flood, leads on to fortune. Omitted, all the voyage of their life is bound in shallows and in miseries. On such a full sea are we now afloat. And we must take the current when it serves, or lose our ventures.

—William Shakespeare, *Julius Caesar*, Act 4, Scene 3

In the blockbuster novel *The Lost Symbol* by Dan Brown, a main character who is a "noetic scientist," a scientist of consciousness, remarks that if all humans could embrace the concept that we are all one with a shared consciousness, despite the appearance of separation, it would change the world overnight. As more and more science reveals, the concept of global oneness is not a fuzzy New Age concept but a fundamental reality. This means that on the most profound and basic level, as great spiritual thinkers from Pythagoras to Gandhi to Ernest Holmes have stated, the fate of one is the fate of all. When one member of God's global family is cut, we all bleed in some way.

Our awareness of this splendid and awesome reality paves the way for a fresh understanding of how we may shed the ugly behaviors and attitudes that come with what seems to be our inherent need to compete with each other economically. From the smallest village in Eastern Europe to the skylines of Manhattan, humans are profoundly driven by an unhealthy desire to prove ourselves worthier, more successful, or wiser than our fellow humans by achieving greater economic success. We compete to acquire more, earn more, spend more, and exhibit more than the next person, company, even church. Religious organizations are hardly immune to this impulse,

THE LAWS OF PROSPERITY

as you can see in some of the grand and even grotesque mega-
churches springing up around the country. They are monuments to
ego, true, but they are more.

They are symbols of our misunderstanding of the interconnect-
edness of our economic nature. The competition, jealousy, and
acquisitiveness that express themselves through our financial lives
are, at heart, the fear that if someone has more than we do, there
will not be enough left for us. We fear being left behind, denied,
found wanting by others who judge us based on how much more we
make or spend than the other guy. We fear being unable to provide
for our families; our concerns magnify until we have become the
sole cause, from our perspectives, of our loved ones' ruin. This has
fueled the most destructive tide of loss and dislocation since the
Great Depression.

The irony is, it's not necessary. When you realize that we are all
one, it becomes clear that we all partake of the same economy and
the same level and strength of monetary energy. When some of us
do well, all of us do well. The saying "a rising tide lifts all boats" has
been applied to trickle-down economics, a discredited economic
theory. In reality, the rising tide applies not to taxes or spending but
to the currency of Mind. When some of us begin to do better, we
enrich the "Mind pool" of intention that exists in the world. This
pool can be considered the collective passive mental energy that has
not yet been consciously applied to the I Am intention and toward
manifesting a specific desire. When we feel wealthy and productive,
the Mind pool grows slightly more positive and prone to producing
abundance. When we feel impoverished, the pool grows more sparse
and more prone to producing greater poverty. So when one does
well, everyone benefits. There is, therefore, no reason to regard
another's wealth, good fortune, or rewarded risk with jealousy, hate,
or spite.

The Law of Rising Tide

All are one, so the increase in prosperity of one enriches the Mind pool of passive intention and makes further wealth easier for all.

The Mind pool is a mighty and startling concept. It is basically our global consciousness, something revealed as reality by the Global Consciousness Project, which shows the increase in order and unified thought around major world events. Think of the pool as a reservoir of unexpressed intention energy slowly trickling from the Minds of each and every conscious being. It is like the background radiation of manifestation: not deliberately used to bring about a desired corporeal result, but subtly shifting the results of manifestation in one direction or another. When a person does deliberately express an I Am intention in order to become a result and bring that result into material existence, she is in part tapping this pool of potential manifestation to shape the outcome. So the pool is like an ever-present power source for Divine Mind, created by us all. When George Lucas presented his idea of the Force in the movie *Star Wars*, he unwittingly described the Mind pool.

The pool is at its heart fundamentally neutral. Since billions around the world are at any time engaged in thoughts ranging from the impoverished to the incalculably rich, the mental energies tend to balance into a neutral state. In this state, the pool does not readily influence the manifestation efforts of anyone very much; results are still based on mental discipline and spiritual strength. But when a great wave of prosperity strikes, such as during a real estate boom or a Wall Street bull market, the energy suddenly shifts to the positive and a wave of wealth-creating passive energy tilts the balance of the Mind pool toward wealth. Suddenly, this pool does influence intentionality and manifestation. Desired results come more easily and prosperity arrives sooner. This is the reason that success appears contagious; when Mind "infects" the world with hope and abundance, barriers to wealth creation drop.

Of course, the converse is also true: when the overarching attitude of a city, a country, or the entire global civilization is bent on poverty and want, this can shift the pool toward the negative and harm intentions for wealth and abundance. Lack is also contagious and the dropping tide can beach some boats that contain otherwise strong, godly intentions of those trying to start businesses, build on inventions, create empires, and change their communities. We are primarily concerned with the effect of the rising tide here, so that remains the focus of our discussion.

CELEBRATE

The underlying message of this Law is this: celebrate your neighbor's good fortune even if it seems that you cannot share it. Revel in the well-being and happiness of others. Consciousness considerations aside, there is a very practical reason for this: it makes you feel wonderful. But have you ever wondered why that is? It is because the more positive thought we project into the Mind pool, the more the pool buoys our own Spirits—and *Spiritus Mundi*. But as to the larger stage, the good of others eases your path to your own beneficial manifestation. If you are maintaining the mental discipline and surety of thought to become the business that you wish to start, greater wealth in your community will increase the pool of positive manifestation energy for Spirit to use in bringing your manifestation into your physical experience.

There are also the more prosaic aspects of this trickle-down effect to take into account. The prosperity of others can create new jobs, make more available money for loans, and bring into your circle new people with experience and connections. So the rising tide effect works in multiple ways, spiritual and physical, to elevate us all, no matter how far removed we are from the good fortune of others. Time and space have no meaning to the power of Spirit.

The lowest ebb is the turn of the tide.

—Henry Wadsworth Longfellow

Four Ways to Make Rising Tide Stronger

Even with the incredible effects of others' prosperity on your own prospects, there are four subtle yet effective ways you can make this power even more beneficial to your own life:

1. **Assist the person who has received the good fortune.** A wise farmer who was desperately poor once decided to assist a prosperous farmer in bringing in his crops when that farmer's son fell ill. Touched by the generosity of the poor man's offer, the farmer agreed. Together, the two men worked for seven days to harvest all the corn, wheat, and vegetable crops and store them safely. When the work was done, the prosperous farmer offered the poor man payment, but the man merely answered, "The only payment I ask is some seed to spread on my own land." The wealthy farmer said that it was too late in the season for the seed to grow; it would just be eaten by birds. But the poor farmer insisted, and the wealthy man paid him in corn and vegetable seeds. The poor farmer went back to his meager land and planted

the seeds. To everyone's surprise, the following month was the warmest and most temperate fall anyone in the region could recall, with sun and rain in perfect proportion. The poor farmer's crop grew with astonishing speed, and he was able to harvest before winter came, guaranteeing his family a well-fed winter.

When you want to speed the results of your own intention, assist someone who is enjoying the kind of prosperity you wish for. So when your small company is struggling and you know someone whose company is thriving, offer to help that entrepreneur handle a busy period, train new staff, or work on his physical location. You will add to the Mind pool precisely the kind of thought that will improve your own manifestation.

2. **Meditate on your own intention.** Since rising tide is a phenomenon of Mind, working on generating prosperous mental energies can only help improve your financial prospects. Spend one hour each day on prosperity meditation, quieting your Mind of all other thoughts and focusing only on those that visualize your great abundance to come and project impressions of plenty and opportunity into the ether. Doing this will gradually train your mind to concentrate on prosperity even when you are not in a meditative mode, expanding your positive effect on the Mind pool. This is a monk-like discipline that will help you in every aspect of your manifestation.

It even offers a greater benefit: your meditation will not only improve the power of your intention and enrich the pool around you, it will help encourage the greater prosperity of others, which in turn will enhance your own opportunity to experience abundance. This is a positive feedback loop that, person by person, spreads wealth and hope and Divine purpose through the entire world.

3. **Help others reverse their misfortune.** Another way to increase the benefit you experience from the Mind pool is to actively engage with others who are suffering from poverty and help them reverse their own situations. The more practical benefits of this sort of service are apparent: the satisfaction of helping others, enriching your community, gaining positive new relationships, and learning. But in terms of spiritual vibration, this is powerful medicine. Helping others discover their own path to prosperity changes the nature and timbre of economic energy flooding into the pool. This reversal can have a galvanic effect on your own attempts to manifest wealth and even on your passive thought processes.

If you are not actively trying to manifest anything at this time, even the act of helping someone else will shift the frequency of your passive, nonmanifestation thought that is flowing into the pool. This thought does exert a pull on the etheric system of manifestation, and it can color what you bring into your orbit before you even try to bring about a conscious change in your future. A transformed pool of personal thought can attract new people, peace and focus of mind, improved health, and sharper perceptions, all assets when the time comes that you are prepared to unleash your own irresistible Mind on the world.

4. **Launch your own efforts after others have achieved wealth.** In other words, don't worry about missing the boat. Do not worry about the trends; the genuine opportunities come after a leading few have sent a rush of positive, prosperous thought into the Mind pool. That is when you should set forth your own I Am intention, riding on that wave of prosperous mental energy. The desire to "be one of the first" is a product more of ego than of

necessity; we want bragging rights. But what does the great risk taker sometimes reap? Ruin, of course. How much better to sit back and wait for others' success to foster a mental environment where your own success becomes much more certain.

The fortunate side effect of this law is that we create a more supportive and mutually joyful environment in which the good of the many and the good of the one are seen as interconnected. Envy, class hatred, and mindless competition serve no purpose other than to inflame passions and create poisonous resentment. We see enough of that in our society as it is. But what if the rich have simply mastered a set of mental tools that enable them to create their own unending flow of opportunity? The Law of Rising Tide is one of those tools.

Certainly, nothing is served by bias and anger directed at those who have brought wealth into their lives. Such individuals give much back to the community: according to Bank of America, even with charitable giving reduced due to the deep recession, the wealthiest American families still gave an average of $54,016 to charitable causes in 2009, donating 9 percent of their total income.[1] These are not the acts of a greedy elite but of people who care for their fellows and know that to give and help others rise in station is to sow the seeds of their own continued success. That is what rising tide is all about, wishing well on others in order to help yourself. It is "enlightened self-interest." As the Bible says in 1 Corinthians 10:24, "Let no man seek his own, but every man another's wealth."

---

1. Margaret Collins, Alexis Leondis, "Charitable Donations by Wealthy Fall 35%, Bank of America Says," November 9, 2010, http://www.bloomberg.com/news/2010-11-09.charitable-donations-by-wealthy-in-u-s-falls-32-bank-of-america-reports.html (accessed April 2011).

The Wealth-Minded Benefit Most from the Rising Tide

You would think that the poor would benefit most from the acquisition of wealth by others because they have the most to gain in raw terms; an increase of $5,000 in annual income means nothing to a millionaire but can be a huge jump in standard of living for someone in poverty. Yet this is not the case. Yes, the poor can see some gifts as the Mind pool tilts toward greater abundance, but because poverty is a state of Mind, they typically see small gains. Remember, those whose Minds dwell on want and lack will manifest that in their lives, so the results of global prosperity will spark their increased fortunes in small ways only.

No, the people who benefit most are those with wealthy Minds. Wealthy thoughts are not limited to those with abundant financial resources but also to those who are rich in the other fruits of life: health, relationships, creativity, and more. You will also find such Spirits as hopeful and positive entrepreneurs and individuals who always seem to find the riches in any situation. To speak plainly, those who will reap the finest harvest from the rising tide will be those who always see good fortune and abundance in their futures. Their positive mental energies will tap the inflow of wealth intention from the rising tide and turn it into rich results. So it pays to train your mind in optimism and in seeing the great potential in any situation.

The Perception of a Rising Tide Can Be Deceptive

There also exist false rising tides, when it seems like others are benefiting from increased wealth and then things take a turn toward darkness. One example of this would be those who purchased homes at inflated prices just prior to the real estate market's collapse. One day they appeared to be part of a rising tide of booming value; the next, they were drowning. The risk of a false rising tide is not that you will not benefit from wishing others well or from maintaining a wealth-oriented Mind. It is that you will assume that you have your own reward coming soon, then become discouraged when it does not come and abandon your mental discipline.

In an article, economist Paul Krugman addressed this mentality when it comes to the global economy and illustrated our same situation well:

> *During a forum held in Seoul, Krugman, the 2008 Nobel Economics laureate and a professor at Princeton University, attributed the current rebound in the global economy to companies quickly selling the inventory accumulated during the worst of the crisis. Thus, government efforts to boost the economy should continue, he said.*
>
> *"The bounce back should not be taken as an indication of continuing growth in manufacturing exports," Krugman said while addressing the World Knowledge Forum hosted by Maeil Business News. "It's too early to say Korea has [achieved] a rapid recovery because world demand, which drives the Korean recovery, will not be sustained," he said.*
>
> *The Korean economy grew 2.6 percent in the second quarter, its fastest growth in five and a half years, with industrial output rising for the second straight month in August from a year earlier. Yesterday, the National Statistical Office released improved employment data, marking the second consecutive one-year job increase.*

However, Krugman said much of the recovery was not attributable to a rebound in global demand, which he said is still in the doldrums. A second recession, the dreaded "double dip," could hit the global economy next year, and on a more serious scale than expected, the economist warned.

That was the reason Krugman warned against quickly ending current expansionary policies. The global economy will take years to fully recover and putting the brakes on the stimulus too early could bring about disastrous results, he said.

"[It's] alarming the large rising tide of people saying we've done enough, [that it's] time to pursue an exit strategy," he said. Krugman said the implementation of an exit strategy should be delayed until unemployment in the United States falls to 7 percent, which he said will come [soon].[2]

The danger of a false rising tide is that you assume your ship has come in and stop doing the things that make your future prosperity most likely. For this reason, it is best to focus on the process and not worry about the results.

A Falling Tide Promotes Caution

Wealth and poverty are not the polar opposites of one another, just as love and hate are not. In reality, fear—not hate—is the opposite of love. And panic—not poverty—is the opposite of wealth. All material states are the result of mental states, and wealth is the result of a mental state of confidence that wealth itself will come to pass. We cannot ride fear through the gate of a mansion. We must train

---

2. Moon Gwang-lip, "Krugman Warns Against Economic Complacency," *Korea JoongAng Daily*, October 15, 2009, http://joongangdaily.joins.com/article/view.asp?aid=2911309.

our Mind to project the intention of absolute surety that wealth and prosperity are about to be born. In the other direction, poverty is the result of panic and lack of confidence that wealth will ever come. It is a total absence of faith in God's system and in our ability to manifest good fortune. So when the tide begins to pull back in our world, we need not predict poverty for ourselves as long as we can avoid panic and instead act with caution and discretion.

Caution means proceeding with our manifestation and its physical form, but without abandon and with more of a plan in mind. It means we do not shed thoughts of wealth for thoughts of want, but we also do not press ahead as though the spirit world were swimming in abundance intention. It is not. As things become more negative, it becomes harder to find a wave of wealth-creating intention to ride. We must act with more prudence and care in our choices, but act all the same. The lowering tide does not mean poverty to all; many continue to thrive no matter how dark the times. They are those who refrain from the blindness of panic.

THERE IS A TIME TO WISH ILL FORTUNE ON OTHERS

Wishing ill on others seems self-defeating. After all, their experience of greater abundance and the abundant mental wealth that comes with it only enriches your chances of manifesting your own good fortune, does it not? Yes, most of the time that is true. Yet there is one instance in which it is not only permissible to wish ill upon the prosperity of another but it actually serves God's purpose: when that person is gaining wealth by stealing from others.

No one could have blamed anyone for wishing the wrath of God down on the head of Bernard Madoff. The same could be said of the Marcos regime of the Philippines and of many other con artists, kleptocrats, and thieves. People who steal not only violate one of the Ten Commandments but also enrich themselves at the expense of many, many others who are left poorer. If the great benefit of wealth lies in enriching the Mind pool so that we may produce more from our intention, the thief who steals from many thwarts that, leaving numerous others poorer and the pool more meager. This act vibrates with negative repercussions throughout the psychoreactive universe.

It is very permissible to use your Mind to try to bring down the thief, as well as your connections, law enforcement, and your own intelligence. Nothing good can come of damaging others to enhance your own treasury.

It is said that we progress from dependence to independence and finally to interdependence, and that is how we know we have achieved true wisdom. We are all one organism, dependent and interdependent upon one another for our common evolution. As we move forward, let the good outcomes of some be cause for us all to rejoice. The wealth of others does not diminish us, or make us less worthy of the same. The success of a person is not judgment that other people cannot also achieve success. I hope we can surpass our tribal nature and instinct to wish for the downfall of the rich and see them for what they are: bringers of good for the collective.

WHAT WE HAVE LEARNED

- We are all one and share in the same reservoir of mental energy.

- You should celebrate the riches of others as signs that your turn is coming.

- There are four ways to enhance the power of the rising tide.

- The wealthy in mind profit most from the rising tide.

18

THE LAW OF SERVICE

■ ■ ■ ■ ■

CORE PRINCIPLES

- Service to others is a fundamental condition of manifestation.

- Service inverts the painful energies of financial loss.

- Service rebounds upon the person who serves with beneficial effects.

Faith is the first factor in a life devoted to service. Without it, nothing is possible. With it, nothing is impossible.

—**Mary McLeod Bethune, American educator, civil rights leader**

Service is a concept whose time has come in this landscape of financial devastation. The idea of public service as a way to elevate ourselves out of the depression of economic loss and the lack of opportunity that pervades our culture is powerful. Service has long been seen as a path to public regard, personal growth, and professional connectedness. But at its heart, service is a mighty spiritual concept that contains within its selfless dynamics the key to escaping the boom-bust cycle of our lives.

Service comes in many forms, but all have the same energy at their core: the desire to uplift ourselves by uplifting others. Yes, at its heart ordinary service is a selfish impulse, because we often serve in order to gain the rush of good feeling that stems from service. This is why many people volunteer at soup kitchens, teach children to read, or bring meals to the indigent elderly. We crave the sensation of doing good not for its own sake but because we want approval from our community, the self-esteem boost that comes from helping others, and the satisfaction of "doing right."

Yet as you might expect, this brand of service is not only empty in nature but counter to the laws of God. Service for your own sake is akin to healing a man of a wound so he may work on your farm—it is good done for one's own self-interest. This taints the nature of the good act. Service in the Spirit, as defined in God's economy, is an act of pure selflessness with one ultimate goal: to alter the flow of manifestation energy not only for yourself but for everyone within your sphere of influence. True service transforms minds, changes hearts, and serves as a living volume of lessons to the served, reminding them of God's infinite generosity through his economic system.

In the Divine economy, the act of service recalibrates the energy of manifestation, opening the flow for those who serve and those who are served. The reason for this is momentous: *service mirrors the cosmic act of love through which God created us.* The nature of true spiritual service is selflessness for its own sake, and although God ultimately stood to benefit through our evolution on this material plane, his initial reason for creation was quite simple: he was a parent bringing life to his beloved children for our own sake. When we as his offspring in Spirit turn our flesh toward helping other individuals or serving an entire community or cause, we become Creators and the same dynamic comes into play: we birth far more than we intended. Just as God created beings that became his proxies in the corporeal world, we create a new flow of spiritual energies when we act out of love and compassion for others.

The nature of service itself needs to be clarified if we are to learn this lesson. Many will say that service is volunteering, cleaning up beaches, giving money to charities, or running in marathons to benefit cancer victims, and all of those acts are worthwhile, but they miss the point of service. It is not the act that defines true service in the Divine economy, but the intention. Just as we must become that which we wish to manifest when we attract wealth into our lives, in order to deliver true service, we must become compassion. The word *passion* actually means "suffering," so *compassion* means "to be with in suffering." When we perform true service, whatever the act, we share the suffering of another, and by doing so, reduce it. To willingly share another's suffering requires great love. This is why true service elevates us to the level of God and why it releases such powerful energies toward our own enrichment.

> *The service of man is the only means by which you can serve God.*
> —Sri Sathya Sai Baba, Indian guru, philanthropist

HEALING YOUR MENTAL ECOSYSTEM

There are many stories of the power of selfless service, but this one illustrates the humility required and the possible rewards beautifully. It involves a group of brothers and elders who ministered to an isolated Christian community:

A brother who was a recent convert in a small branch in eastern Ukraine was a hardworking father who made very little income from his job but tried diligently to provide for his family. All of his income went to buy food and to pay rent, utilities, and tithing. There was nothing left over for extras. But the one thing this dear brother wanted most of all was a tie to wear to church when he could bless the sacrament.

During the preceding couple of months he had saved a few pennies from each of his paychecks and put the money in a small leather coin purse with the hope that one day he would finally be able to purchase a tie to wear to church. By the week before the fasting and testimony meeting, he had gathered sufficient funds to purchase his tie. He was so excited! Then, in the

middle of the week, a family member became ill, and the saved
tie funds were needed to purchase medicine. This dear brother
was quite disappointed that another Sunday would go by with-
out a tie. The days preceding church he silently prayed that
somehow he could acquire a tie—not an expensive tie, just a
simple, plain tie—so he could respectfully administer the sacra-
ment of the Lord.

Late Saturday afternoon there was a knock at his apart-
ment door, and when he opened the door there stood Elder
Abegglen and his companion. As he gazed down at Elder Abeg-
glen's hands, his eyes locked on a tie the missionary was holding.

"I understand you can use this tie," said Elder Abegglen.
With tears in his eyes, this good brother said, "I am here today
to tell you God knows the simple desires of our hearts, and He
sends forth His servants to answer our prayers."[1]

You are one of those servants. Each of us is. Within each of us
dwell both the duty and the desire to serve. But service is also a
powerful way to transform our personal fortunes, a reason for, in this
terrible economic time, the booming number of Americans working
as volunteers or for service organizations. According to the Volunteering in America 2010 report, approximately 1.6 million more
volunteers served in 2009 than in 2008, the largest single-year increase
in the number of volunteers since 2003.[2] But such service yields no
pay, no immediate new jobs, and no relief from debt or foreclosure.
What do these people know that others do not? They understand the
Law of Service.

---

1. Jo Ann C. Abegglen, "The Power of One: Selfless Service" (address, College of Nursing, Brigham
Young University, Provo, UT, July 11, 2006).

2. http://www.volunteeringinamerica.gov (accessed April 2011).

The Law of Service

*Serving others selflessly alters the dynamic of mental
energy in your world, resulting in the cosmos bowing
to your service in return in the form of richer
and more rewarding manifestation.*

As we have discussed before, those who engage in selfless service know that to serve others is to heal a mental and spiritual ecosystem scarred by loss, fear, debt, poverty, despair, and threats from outside agents. They understand that service is a transformative experience that helps each one who serves evolve into a different and higher being. Think of the qualities that we associate with those who serve their community consistently: patience, generosity, perseverance, love, perspective, gratitude, humor, kindness, hope. Are those not all qualities we should be cultivating as we hope to manifest better lives for ourselves and our families in the future?

This is the secret behind service and why it is such a powerful force, especially in hard times. As we have discussed, we live in a universe of manifestation—the mental transforming the spiritual into the material. Everything that flows into our conscious present from the future comes as a result not just of how we think but of who we become, the constant state of our Body, Mind, and Spirit. In trying to manifest greater abundance, security, opportunity, health, love, and peace, when we become superior human representatives of those qualities, we manifest them in greater quality and quantity. The true power of selfless service lies in its power, through the act of serving, to transform those of us serving into beings who live more in line with the finest qualities God wishes us to manifest.

Service helps us become beings who can better manifest good fortune for ourselves—and in turn, help others do the same.

Service to others exerts a healing force on the ecosystem of your life and the world around you. It balances the negative energies that so often infect your Mind and surroundings when difficult times strike. The act of serving pulls us out of that deeply introspective state that can become depressive and manifest further poverty; it expands our vision and shifts our eyes to what can be and grants us power to change circumstances at a time when we may feel powerless. Compassion and giving to others are virtually all-powerful in their potency to transform the beings we are into the beings we can become and shift Minds to a state that is more fruitful, more able to manifest wonders. Their popularity speaks to their ability to turn around economic troubles by "resetting" the Mind in a direction of uplift and hope, states conducive to attracting economic good.

Service to others is the rent you pay for your room here on earth.
—Shirley Chisholm, congresswoman, educator, author

THE FOUR PRINCIPLES OF SERVICE

The nature of service seems simple, but as I have said, self-concerned service and the spiritual service that transforms and creates in the mode of God are different in nature. Spiritual service is based on four philosophical pillars:

1. **It must be purely selfless.** You cannot go into a serving act with the intention of making yourself look better to your peers, improving your standing in the community, networking for job offers or opportunities, or making up for past sins. The self-interest in such motivations is self-evident and the insecurity

and greed they represent counter any transformative effects. True service that transforms you must be undertaken with the intent to transform others.

2. **It must be teaching.** The old maxim about "teaching a man to fish and feeding him for life" remains profound wisdom. Ideal service should not just be about aid but about transforming others into beings more in line with the Divine ideal. When you can both serve and teach, whether by design or example, you further enrich the mental landscape around you and make it more fertile for your own manifestation.

3. **It must be generational.** You must attempt to inspire the individuals you serve to in turn serve others, moving the wave of service into future generations. This dynamic expands the circle of service like the ripples from a stone thrown in a pond, spreading it wider and wider and further enriching the mental ecosystem that produces wealth.

4. **It must be timely.** No one needs assistance recovering from a flood during the dry season. Service must come when others need it, not when it is convenient for the person providing the service. Rendering assistance in love to someone who needs it is noble, but if it comes too late or meets a need that does not exist, it is futile. Those who wish to change the world with their service should be aware of the tides of service and how those tides affect the needs of others, the community, and the world at large.

Service of others remains one of the most holy and spiritual of all acts. The selfless aid of another, even at one's own expense, goes back to Abraham, the father of Christianity, Judaism, and Islam. When he sought to sacrifice his son Isaac to God, Abraham was in the state of service—meeting the needs of another (in this case, the need of God for his absolute obedience) while potentially harming himself, as he doubtlessly would have been harmed had he actually slaughtered his child. This is always the core instinct behind true spiritual service: putting others over self, giving over receiving, creating plenty for others as its own reward, because the act of righteousness in the face of God is pleasurable without any further enhancement.

Yet there is a delicate balance that must be struck in the act of serving if one is to reap the incredible rewards of service. On one hand, this is a book about rising from your own economic hard times, and service is certainly a potent tool for manifesting greater fortunes. On the other, as I have said, the spiritual service that transforms us into beings who can then attract greater abundance must be purely selfless. How then to maintain this delicate balance? How can we serve others with no interest in reward or profit dwelling in our minds but also know that if we provide such pure godlike compassion and love, we will indeed manifest greater rewards? Is that not hypocrisy?

It need not be. It is a personal act of great mental discipline to know that your selfless service will help you personally in the future while maintaining the purity of intention that makes the service selfless. It is as though we must intentionally forget, or practice some kind of Orwellian doublethink, in order to serve with complete concern only for the needs of others while not letting the knowledge of our own benefit taint our intention. Doing this means placing your knowledge of service and its power not in your Mind but deep in your Spirit, where it will be accessible only through deep meditation or prayer. The danger of storing this knowledge in the Mind is that it can appear through normal cognition and sabotage your efforts.

I relate this to the process by which we become fit through exercise. The long-term goal may be fitness and health, but if we focus on that goal, we may lose the motivation to do the immediate work that in the short-term can be painful and difficult. Similarly, we must cherish the process of service for the act of being compassionate and godlike without any conscious thought of the rewards it may bring via physical manifestation. This demands a mental discipline as great as the discipline required to maintain the I Am intention for our desires when we work to manifest wealth, a home, or a business.

It can take years to develop such strong control of your conscious and unconscious Mind, but without it, the act of service can be less effective in changing your personal fortunes.

Service Can Yield Blessings Even after Self-Concerned Thoughts

There is a question as to how much conscious thought of the benefit you might receive from an act of service is enough to sabotage the enhancement of your own manifestation that might result from that service. The answer is: it varies with each soul. If you are engaged in some kind of service to others that began as selfless, but then thoughts creep into your Mind about how wonderful it will be when you receive your Divine reward for what you are doing, have you instantly ruined your future manifestation? Some damage has been done, but the reduced wealth that your Mind produces in your experience is proportionate to the persistence of your selfish thought. The longer your thoughts of selfish reward endure, the more they deplete the manifestation energy that will enrich what you will experience in the future. Stopping selfish thoughts early, like finding a tumor when it is small, increases the chance of minimizing damage.

The safest way to proceed, should you succumb to the very human tendency to think—at least in part—about all the good that will come your way when the cosmos rewards you, is to remind yourself to be cognizant of the joys of the process. Remember that the act of serving in itself brings you closer to God and pure Spirit. Nothing is more indicative of the Divine than one man reaching out to help a stranger. You can get your intention back on track by diving deep into the process of service and savoring its tang and flavor. Thoughts of reward will retreat.

SERVICE RENDERED FOR SELFISH REASONS IS NOT WORTHLESS

Service in any form is never without benefit. The question is, does selfish service benefit you, the server, in any way? Yes, of course it does. It simply may not enrich and enhance the quality, quickness, or character of what you manifest later in your life through the interaction of your Divine Mind with the psychoreactive universe. But even if you go into an act of service for reasons that are entirely selfish, such as to receive the approbation of the community, there are still benefits. Service, like love, has no dark side.

First of all, even if you do not improve future fortunes via a selfless, spiritual service, you may still learn new skills, get a clearer perspective on the good fortune of your own life, or establish fruitful new personal relationships. You may learn patience, wisdom, and healing. Second, assisting others for any reason enriches the Mind pool that we discussed earlier, which in turn does help your own manifestation. Finally, service inspires others to emulate you and serve selflessly in the name of God and Christ, thereby helping transform poor communities, bringing services to those who need them, improving local economies, and improving the future for everyone. Service should always be undertaken for any reason.

Dwell on the Reward Only when the Service Is Complete

It is acceptable to think about reward after you have completed your act of selfless service. Once the act is done, you have projected great compassion and Divine purity into the cosmos, and that cannot be reversed, so it will affect your future manifestation in a positive way. Ideally, we should not dwell on reward at all and live purely in the light of selflessness, but that is simply not realistic for most of us. We remain human beings with our inherent and inherited weaknesses, one of which is the anticipation of pleasure. So while the ideal would be pure lifelong selflessness, completing the act and then thinking about how it will benefit you will not damage your fortunes.

Still, prudence is called for. To complete your service one day and the next to become obsessed with greed over how you can turn that experience into riches beyond measure is to go a great length toward sabotaging the entire good work. Remember, the act of selfless service is beneficial because it is transformative; we become more the beings who can manifest great good from Divine Mind. If we change from selfless to utterly selfish in a heartbeat, we project great hypocrisy into the cosmos and can undo all that we have done. The safest road is to briefly enjoy the reward you might receive but not to cross over into the ugly emotion of entitlement. Instead, take satisfaction in the knowledge that you have become greater, wiser, and more giving, and have faith that reward will come. Then move on to your next act of service.

There have never been so many opportunities to serve our fellows as now. There are international organizations, national groups, government service coalitions, charities, schools, environmental groups—the list is endless. But it is perhaps wisest to reach out and try to find ways to serve within your own community or your own church. There you will not only find as many people in need as through Habitat for Humanity or the Peace Corps but people whose welfare means more to you, because they dwell under the eyes of God right in your backyard.

The act of service should be joyful and relevant to you in your own life today, without even considering what can come tomorrow. As Charles Fillmore, the cofounder of Unity, said, "We shall serve for the joy of serving, prosperity shall flow to us and through us in unending streams of plenty."[3] He was talking not only about financial prosperity but the prosperity of the Body and Mind and Spirit. Service to a cause greater than one's own narrow needs can become the great purpose of life, as it does for many. There is perhaps no Law with more potential to transform our world in every conceivable manner.

WHAT WE HAVE LEARNED

- Service heals the wounds of economic crisis.

- There are four keys to true selfless service.

- Balancing selflessness with the knowledge of reward demands great discipline.

- Service in any form is always beneficial.

---

3. http://thinkexist.com (accessed August 21, 2009).

19

THE LAW OF THE CONTRACT

■   ■   ■   ■   ■

CORE PRINCIPLES

- Your existence is an implied contract with God to be his proxy on earth.

- It is also an implied contract that you will adhere to God's economic laws.

- Manifestation requires that you fulfill the terms of a contract you can only know via prayer.

Society is indeed a contract. It is a partnership in all science, a partnership in all art, a partnership in every virtue and in all perfection ... between those who are living, those who are dead and those who are to be born.

—Edmund Burke, British statesman, philosopher

The contract is a fundamental underpinning of human society, but there is the temptation to attribute it to the machinations of a group of attorneys. This is false; the contract goes back much, much further, to the original covenant between God and humankind and back even to the Creation. However, the concept of the binding contract is built upon a basic and irrefutable cosmic principle that underlies all human relations: the idea that a promise can be trusted and a covenant will be honored. There is a reason a mortgage is called a "first trust deed"; the arrangement implies that the borrower will repay the debt according to the terms of the contract. Once again, the nature of money invades even the most basic of human interactions, need and trust.

Trust is at the heart of all human societies. We trust that our parents will raise us and protect us. We trust that our spouse will remain faithful. We trust that people will be good and just and not steal from us. We trust that our games are straight, our builders have done their jobs properly in erecting our skyscrapers and bridges, and our doctors are advising us according to our needs and not their desire to earn greater income. Without trust made formal and ritualistic by the forms and functions of the law, the civilized society that has brought us so many wonders would find it extremely difficult to function.

But the idea of the contract is more than a piece of paper, in much the same way that money is not just currency or the balance in your online banking system. Just as money is the tangible representation of a gigantic idea—the Divine power of change in the material world—the contract is the physical proxy for the inherent agreement between Creator and Created and between the co-Created. When God crafted the first human beings and set up the laws of his economic system to reward those who evolved with the greatest wisdom and discipline, a contract was also put into force. I call it the Covenant, but the idea is the same. The Covenant states this as the duty of every man and woman: *that you shall labor to the best of your ability to evolve in Mind and Spirit to the highest form possible, returning to your Source with all the wisdom you can bring to your Father.*

This is the essence of our reason for existence: God created us as his representatives in the material plane. God is pure Spirit and so cannot directly interact with this reality; he must do so through us. We are, therefore, God pressed out into this world. This is a titanic gift, but it does not come free. We are not allowed to receive life without the expectation of payback. In return for his great goodness, God demands of each of us that we grow and evolve in wisdom, strength, compassion, love, and knowledge of him, and that when we leave this life to return to Spirit, we bring with us the lessons we have learned. In this way does God himself evolve. Each of us carries with us in Spirit an infinitesimal piece of the evolving energy of God. To provide that energy is what the Covenant, our contract, stipulates.

When we promise to love, we really mean that we promise to honor a contract.

—Anthony Burgess, English novelist, critic

Payment for Services Rendered

This broad contract with God, built on trust, implies that we cannot simply fritter away our lives without consequences. To do so is to default on the great debt of self-evolution that we owe God. But the contract goes to a level deeper than this. Not only is it a lasting and inherent contract in human existence that was passed down to us from the first human beings, a contract comes into being each time we declare an I Am intention and begin to manifest a desire into corporeal existence. The universe is a sphere of transactions, one into another, between our continuously changing energies and the eternal nature of the Lord and his system.

The Law of The Contract

When you consciously manifest a desired result into existence, you also sign a contract with God to fulfill certain conditions. Fail and your manifestation will be tainted in form.

In human affairs, virtually any transaction features the inherent and seamless introduction of a contract of trust in conduct (this could also have been called the Law of Transaction), though we are often unaware of it. When you buy something with a credit card, you are signing a contract to pay the temporary loan. When you board a bus or plane, you are tacitly agreeing to a contract of carriage that spells out the transport system's obligations and liabilities. When you park your car, you agree to a contract. When you marry, you agree to a contract of conduct. Contracts based on trust—and the need to protect against the unexpected—saturate our society. They are everywhere.

So, too, are unseen but very real contracts built into the machinations of Divine Mind and the cosmic economy. When you take in hand your intention and declare in Divine Mind that "I Am a new job that pays me twice what I made at my old job," you are setting formidable wheels in motion. Among them are, of course, the wheels that will gradually manufacture your result in Spirit and deliver it into your tangible experience, but you also set in motion a legal aspect of God's economy. Implied in any I Am intention are certain covenants of mental and spiritual conduct that you must fulfill if you wish to receive the result you desire in a way that benefits you. These conditions are:

- You will maintain strong mental discipline to continue to focus the cosmic energies on your desire, acting and thinking as though your desire is already realized in order to press out that same result from your thought.
- You will continue to evolve beyond the fulfillment of your desire so that it becomes not an end to your aspirations but a beginning. So, if you manifest a new company, when that manifestation is achieved, according to your contract you must continue to grow your vision into something larger or something that serves a greater good, not merely sit on your profits in self-satisfaction.
- You will use whatever you manifest to serve a cause larger than yourself—by improving your community, creating jobs, becoming a leader or officeholder, or some other purpose.
- You will improve your life to be worthy of the gifts of manifestation by taking steps like ridding your life of poisonous relationships, overcoming addictions, healing rifts with

loved ones, or increasing your store of personal knowledge through education or mentorship.

HIDDEN CLAUSES

These are the basic conditions of any contract with God—the Lord's boilerplate, we might say. However, as with any agreement of trust, there can be more. There may be hidden clauses in your contract with God, conditions that you must meet that will also affect the results of your manifestation. You must know them to fulfill them; not to do so will cause great harm to the result you are working to bring into your conscious life. So how can you discover any hidden conditions that exist in your contract? Through meditation and prayer.

It is always wise to meditate or pray as a regular part of your spiritual discipline. Just as daily exercise is a vital component of one's physical well-being, regular meditative contact with the universe is an important aspect of spiritual fitness. This is never more critical than when one is in the early stages of manifesting a specific desire from the etheric plane. When you first declare your I Am intention, follow that with a regular discipline of undisturbed meditation or prayer in which you clear your Mind of all distractions and open it to the Voice of God. In these sessions, God will reveal to you any other conditions beyond the four basic ones that he wishes you to meet in order to fully manifest your desire.

He will reveal these conditions to you in visions. You may suddenly see in your Mind's eye a nonprofit agency attached to the business you are trying to manifest; you will know that is something God wishes you to create. You may have the overpowering urge to build a music studio as part of the mansion that you desire; that is God telling you that when your fine home manifests, you will have cause to use music to work his will, so you'd better have the facilities to do so. God may reveal one hidden clause to you or half a dozen, but the course is clear: listen, see, heed, and follow. Each condition is necessary for God's system to completely fulfill your intention to the letter.

A marvelous example of this principle in action was the work of a financial planner who set forth into the universe a powerful desire to improve his career, which had been solely focused on money and left him feeling empty, his family neglected, and his life in chaos. He put forth the intention of having a richer, more rewarding, more holistic career but was not more specific than that; in his faith, he trusted God's system to move him in the direction that best served God. In his meditation, he also found a hidden condition: in order for his vision to manifest fully, the financial planner would have to become a speaker as well. He was called by God to get up before hundreds of his colleagues and speak to them about how to improve their professional lives. He had always wanted to speak, but in his relentless pursuit of high income had never done it. So he followed the vision sent to him and began speaking to groups of financial professionals around the country.

As the months passed, something he did not expect happened: speaking became an overwhelming passion for him. He did it more and more, and as he did, his work as a financial planner suffered. But he was a huge hit as a speaker; more and more of his colleagues responded to the passion for a better life that he brought to his speeches. Slowly it began to dawn on him: this was the more satisfying life of passion and service he had tried to manifest, even though he had not expected this. Clearly, speaking was his purpose. So in a leap of great faith, he scaled back and eventually abandoned his financial practice, wrote a book, and began speaking throughout the country about how financial professionals can transform their careers to be richer, more enjoyable, and more in line with their character and values. Because he discovered God's hidden condition in the cosmic contract and followed it without hesitation, he manifested a result he could never have imagined but that transformed his life into a moving blessing.

Contracts make us nervous. Even when we are sure that we're getting the best deal or agreeing to conditions that we can definitely fulfill, we still feel a pang of anxiety, a need to glance over our shoulders. We're committing to something that can be life altering, and it makes us doubt ourselves. And that's when we're forging an agreement with a lender or an employer. What must we feel when entering into a binding contract with the Creator of the universe? If we thought about it, we would doubtlessly feel overwhelmed. But it is important to remember that God is not trying to trip us up. He wants us to succeed, to be rich, to live on an estate, to have no more financial worries, to work at what thrills us, to have health and love, and to give to others.

God's contracts are drawn up with the most lenient terms possible and the loosest enforcement. We are allowed to make mistakes, fall down, and fail temporarily with no penalty; God knows that such errors are part of our learning experience. So there is no need to fear a covenant with the Lord as long as you enter it with an open heart and true intentions to fulfill the conditions. God is not going to condemn you for the slightest shortcoming; his system will reward you for the effort as much as for the result, because you are human and therefore imperfect. Remember, manifestation is about intention and becoming. Working with pure and true intention to become what God wishes you to be carries a great deal of weight in the court of the cosmos. So sign your contract with the Lord without anxiety. As long as you enter with honor, you are safe.

All sensible people are selfish, and nature is tugging at every contract to make the terms of it fair.
—Ralph Waldo Emerson, *The Conduct of Life*

MEET THE CONTRACT'S CONDITIONS

It is a simple truth that if you should enter into a covenant with the deliberate intention of spitting in God's eye and ignoring any or all of the conditions, you will experience great misfortune. This is not about trying and failing to maintain strong mental discipline; as I said, effort and true intent matter. But when you thumb your nose at the debt that a Divine contract implies, you will still manifest that which you have set in motion, but it will be in a form that either falls far short of your desire or that actually harms your long-term vision for your life.

Perhaps you sign the trust deed for a new home with a mortgage payment that you can realistically afford and have every intention of paying your debt and fulfilling the contract terms. But through no fault of your own, you lose your job and are unable to make the mortgage payments. If you have exhibited good intentions and have worked to fulfill the contract as best you could, you are far more likely to find yourself treated with tolerance and justice as you try to work things out. Your lender will be more likely to help you, and government agencies may assist you as well. Your intent of honor and desire to be trustworthy carry great weight.

However, if you sign the contract with a blatant disregard for your debt, you will be treated like a criminal and deserve to be treated as such. In showing yourself unworthy of trust, you create a future of punitive measures: litigation, bankruptcy, homelessness, even jail. Thus is it with God. If you refuse to comply with your conditions, you may find your manifestation only partially materializing.

For example, a desired new home may come to pass but turn out to be seriously defective. Or you may manifest something actively damaging to your life, such as a new relationship that turns out to destroy all of your other relationships. The more clauses of the Divine contract that you disregard, the more your manifestation will be distorted and destructive.

Getting Out of Your Contract with God

Can you get out of a contract to purchase a home or marry a person once you have signed it? Yes, but only with great difficulty, pain, and expense. A contract with God is even more irreversible; once you set the gears of manifestation in motion, it is virtually impossible to stop them. Even if you abandon your intention five minutes after stating your I Am, you are in line for something to come into your experience as it becomes corporeal and the stream of time pulls you toward it in your future.

If you realize your folly, the best you can do once you hold that powerful I Am thought in your Divine Mind and declare it to the Universe is to immediately abandon any thoughts or actions you were taking to become that which you desired to manifest. Since the creation engine of the Universe will mirror the person you become in bringing you your desire, if you become a being far different from the person you intended to become when you stated your intention, you will probably see little manifestation of consequence. This is a circumstance where the leniency of God is truly a blessing; he will not take you to great task for an intention that was not your deepest desire. There is little good to be had by exercising punitive action for what may have been a momentary whim or a "thought of passion." If you cease all thought and action in the direction of your manifestation, you may notice no result at all. If you do, it should not impact you in a very negative way.

However, such incidents should always be cautionary: the I Am intention is the most powerful force imaginable and should never be employed without the strongest conviction.

THE NEED FOR BALANCE

As we have discussed, the cosmos maintains balance in all things, and this reflexive mechanism includes the balance between that which is granted through manifestation and that which is given by each of us in payment for our gift. This necessitates a contract between us and God—not because God does not trust us, but because a mandate to enforce the yin-yang balance of forces is woven into the DNA of the cosmos.

This is why your manifestation will mirror your self-improvement, mental discipline, selflessness, and vision, in addition to your ability to fulfill any other conditions God has set for you as discovered through meditation and prayer. The energies that you present during the period when your manifestation is slowly brewing toward fruition in the cosmic machinery directly shape the final result that you experience, and this is the nature of the contract. The other reason that God requires a contract is that ours is a cosmos built on predictable laws, not chaos. The laws of Divine Mind and Prosperity are not in effect one moment and then nullified the next. As with the laws of humanity, they are always in effect unless repealed, and only God can repeal one of his own Laws.

The need for the contract does not imply that God does not trust us. Contracts enforce rules that protect and reward those with the honor and trust to commit to fulfilling their conditions. Should someone who requests a gift from God's system and then ignores its price receive the same blessing as one who thinks, lives, and becomes according to God's will? No. The Law of the Contract is one of cosmic fairness and justice.

SPIRITUAL ADVISERS ARE GOD'S ATTORNEYS

When you wish to interpret the meaning of a contract, you contact an attorney. When you wish to discover the hidden meaning of a clause in a covenant with God, you contact a prophet or other spiritual adviser. The prophet, through his or her disciplined Mind and ability to capture and recognize the Voice of God that speaks to all of us, is uniquely gifted to help you uncover and translate the meaning of any vision, passion, or impulse that you feel is related to the manifested desire you have stated to the cosmos.

The spiritual adviser fills the same vital role that an attorney fills in human society: he or she speaks the language of God's laws. God does not speak to us in the way that you and I speak, for his messages cannot be contained in mere words. Instead, when you are in the heart of your meditation and discovering the hidden requirements that God asks of you, you will find sharp visions, angelic voices, powerful sudden passions, lightning-bright ideas that seem to come from nowhere—the language of inspiration, dreams, and fiery passion. You will feel driven, compelled to act on these communications. But are they part of your contract with God or something from your own mind? If you are unsure, then communion with a prophet or adviser can help you find the answers.

Any adviser is only an interpreter. Like an earthly attorney, they are subject to the rulings of a judge, and only God is the judge in these matters. A truthful prophet will not speak in absolutes but in guidance and clear judgment; the decision to act will remain yours based on your personal connection to God.

Do not fear God's contracts. Rather, celebrate them. Their true purpose is to ennoble you and to give you the incentive to grow and enrich your Mind and Spirit so that you become worthy of the gifts you have asked the Divine system to bestow upon you. As any earthly economist will tell you, economics is primarily about incentives, factors that provide fiscal motivation to take or not take action: price discounts, No Parking signs, late fees, frequent flyer miles. Incentives are proven to drive human action; we all respond to them. But where did our inspiration for them come from? From God's economy, of course.

God's economic system incentivizes us to evolve, to become wiser and more selfless and to listen to our inner Minds in prayer. Remember that God wants us to be wildly successful and to achieve every iota of our dreams, but to reach that pinnacle, he knows that we must be motivated. Hence the contract that compels dedicated action. It is the same with human contracts: would so many people own their own homes without the compulsion to pay a mortgage created by the lending contract? Of course not. Many people would spend their money frivolously if not forced by penalty of law to pay a small sum each month. Contracts focus us and drive us to disciplined improvement. They are one of God's great wisdoms.

What We Have Learned

- God's contracts exist to give you incentives to better yourself.

- They also exist to reward those who fulfill their duty to God.

- Once a contract is signed with the Universe, it must be carried out.

- The spiritual adviser is your attorney with God.

20

THE LAW OF VALUES

■　　■　　■　　■　　■

CORE PRINCIPLES

- Values communicate who you are to others.

- Only values will inspire others to become enlightened as you are—that is the Great Commission.

- Your values will drive your income.

Maturity is achieved when a person postpones immediate pleasures for long-term values.

—Joshua Loth Liebman, expert in psychiatry and religion

Family values, societal values, conservative values, liberal values—these are catchall terms that may have validity as political tools but mean nothing in our discussion of the evolving Mind. This shorthand offers merely labels used to manipulate what cynical movers see as gullible people; pay no attention to them. Instead, full and true values lie at the center of the motivational forces that guide every conscious being in the world. You are your values. They represent your character and your views, the barometer of your tolerance, and the lodestone of your ethics. Your values are unique to you but are God-inspired. They are the voice of God speaking to you in your waking life.

Your values are your unconscious telemetry to God, reflecting the microscopic aspect of the infinite Divine Mind that you represent. In that tiny aspect, almost indivisible in its minute size, your values are a sliver of the total conscience of the One God. Remember, you are God pressed out. You share a conscience and spiritual nature with him. So values are not to be belittled as political labels or mechanisms for launching pogroms against perceived enemies. Values are serious business. They are living aspects of Divine Mind.

As such, they cannot be reduced to mere political slogans or marketing jingles. Values are even more than the compasses by which we guide the ships of our lives. They are the very width and breadth of that which makes us more than animals. Our values are the mental shadows of our Spirits. And in the fabric of God's cosmic economy, values are currency for a simple yet indomitable reason: *they communicate the nature of a person's Spirit to other people more clearly than any other single factor.*

The purpose of each human being on this plane is to evolve and bring accumulated material wisdom to the Spirit Consciousness that is God. Therefore, ultimately, the only true reason that God allows us to manifest wealth in this world is ... what? Only through building and changing the world can we inspire other beings to become enlightened themselves—to grow closer to God and discover his Kingdom for what it really is, his economic system. But words cannot communicate the message and Spirit that inspires; as a wise man once said, "Talk is cheap." We see many pious men and women who commit terrible acts and live counter to any values inspired by God. Are these the ones to lead others to enlightenment? No. Actions speak the truth, and actions are always driven by our values. Here is the way that values fit into the equation of your personal prosperity:

1. When you manifest a desire, your results are dictated by the level to which your actions reflect your mental and spiritual maturity and your commitment to serving and inspiring others—your thoughts, words, and actions.

2. Your thoughts, words, and actions are driven by the core values that you hold.

3. Therefore, ultimately, your values will determine what you manifest in the short-term and how that result evolves in the long-term.

THE LAW OF VALUES:

Your values determine how effectively you inspire others to learn God's system and become enlightened, and that in turn impacts the wealth you can manifest.

Your values directly impact how you will attract wealth and prosperity in the end. Values are at the core of all thoughts, or more precisely, all thoughts are screened by your value system. Think about this, for it is vital. Values are the screening factor that determines what thoughts your Spirit allows your Mind to dwell upon. All of us, every man and woman, entertain thoughts of lust, theft, violence and cheating from time to time. It's human. But when such thoughts come into the Mind of a man whose values are centered on justice and honor? He instantly dismisses them as beneath his Spirit. Values are the filter that determine how elevated or debased a human being may be. The values you hold are your eternal and immortal Spirit made manifest in your material Mind, and they speak with a mighty voice.

You perform better when your thoughts, feelings, emotions, goals and values are in balance.

—Brian Tracy, *The Way to Wealth in Action*

THE GREAT COMMISSION

If the purpose given to us by God is to evolve and to inspire others to evolve, then inspiration is our weapon in what is the real Great Commission. This is controversial, but it must be addressed. For generations now, Christians have believed we are called on to convert the unsaved and damn the rest to hell. In doing this, we have created a culture of intolerance for those who do not hew to our narrow interpretation of the Christian faith and placed a vast and frightening burden on the shoulders of young evangelists who feel they are never doing enough. It is time to shed the light of truth on this lie.

The Great Commission is not about conversion. The average evangelist who assails people with words actually creates no more than a handful of true converts in a lifetime. What is the effect? Words convey nothing. Words are easy. Action speaks with the voice of titans! The true Great Commission is for each of us who understands the Mind and economy of God and the true nature of humankind to inspire others to discover what we have learned and to do so through our actions and demonstrable values. Values have incredible power to inspire, to move mountains, and to change the world.

If you doubt that, then think about the people behind these names: Martin Luther King, Jr., Mohandas K. Gandhi, Nelson Mandela, Rosa Parks, Susan B. Anthony, and Anne Frank. People whose simple convictions and the actions that supported them inspired others to such a fury of love, devotion, and passion that they have become immortal symbols of struggle and victory. We are put here to learn this truth and light the way for others to evolve as we are evolving! One day, in the unimaginable future, all humanity will have come into this light, and there will be no more reason for God to maintain this economic system. At that time, he may end this world and bring us all home, or he may construct a new system to meet a new need that cannot be imagined by our meager human minds. He will give us a new Great Commission.

But that is not a time for us to worry about. That would be monumental hubris. We have our system and our challenges today.

Within the bounds of that system, we work to spread the true gospel of the economy of the Lord and our exalted place within it.

Values and Income

But we must return to the matter of money and economic health, as our discussion of prosperity mandates. We are always keeping one eye on the barometer of personal financial survival, a necessity in these hard times. So how do values translate into fiscal health and prosperity? Aren't values a luxury we cannot afford in a time when jobs are scarce and millions are fighting simply to live?

No. Values have never been more important, provided you are operating in God's economy, not the surface economy of the material world. In the economy of intention, I Am declaration, becoming and manifestation, and the spirit and mental state you maintain as you work to manifest your desire into corporeal being determine the abundance you can realize. The closer you are to being the perfect ideal of God's co-Creator—mentally focused purely on creation, oriented on service to others, your Mind already transformed into the mental reality of what you are going to manifest in the physical realm—the greater and richer what you manifest will be.

For example, someone who is powerfully in tune with those requirements and who desires to manifest a new business will likely manifest a company that thrives from the day it opens its doors. Everything will fall into place. Someone who strays from that near-perfection will manifest a business that has more trouble getting off the ground. The more like God you can become, the greater your creative powers will be. And your ability to guide your Mind and spirit in the direction of Creation is motivated by the strength and sureness of your values. The more certain you are of what you serve and the more strongly you feel compelled to serve it, despite temptation and resistance from others, the better you will be at attracting prosperity into your awareness.

So values directly affect your income. What's more, even if you are not completely operating within God's economy, strong adherence to core values, such as honor, courage, compassion, fidelity, sobriety, and learning, will help you be more successful. Such values move people and engender trust in a world where so much is relative and so many people are seen as being unworthy of trust. So even if your evolution into a being of spirit and intention is only beginning, knowing and following your values will help you in creating profitable relationships, finding or keeping a job, and dealing with everyone in your world.

Open your arms to change, but don't let go of your values.
—His Holiness The Dalai Lama

WHAT ARE YOUR VALUES?

And so we come to the question of values. What are yours? Do you know? When we talk about values, people often list spiritual qualities like the ones I cited above. Others commonly listed include:

- Truthfulness
- Trust
- Family
- Independence
- Equality
- Justice
- Healing
- Tolerance
- Self-Sacrifice

These are all wonderful qualities, but they do not answer our question. Your values are not on a list. Your values consist of two categories of ideas:

Ideas or actions you will always stand for.

Ideas or actions you will always stand against.

So if you will always insist on honesty among your family members no matter what the consequences, that is one of your values. If you will never stand for disrespect of an elder, then that is one of your values. If you vacillate on standing for or standing against something, it is not one of your values. This is a simple, elegant gauge of your value system.

Values can also be negative. A person can value drugs or alcohol above other things in life. Someone can believe that honesty is not as important as personal gain. *Values* does not imply that something is a source of light in the eyes of God, but if it is to result in your successful manifestation, it must be. It should be clear by now that intentions based on greed, violence, or envy manifest only results based on those values. They will make of your life hell.

Your values are the absolute guiding stars of your life in a world of relative movements and actions. They rarely change once you become an adult and a parent. Your values are your Spirit pressed out into the conscious world that does not require prayer or meditation for you to communicate with it. That is why they inspire: Spirit talks to Spirit even if the Mind does not understand. Know your values and you will know what to be guided by as you evolve into a co-Creator through your power to manifest your desires.

Aesop, the Greek purveyor of fables, said, "Don't let your special character and values, the secret that you know and no one else does, the truth—don't let that get swallowed up by the great chewing complacency."[1] What a wonderful phrase, the great chewing complacency. It is easy to become complacent about our values in this world because we are so often told that they are anachronisms. They don't matter. And yet, if we are to achieve the great wealth that changes lives and gives us the power to reach out and transform the world, our values are the gateway. Values move Minds and civilizations. So as we conclude this final chapter about our last Law, let us examine some aspects of our values.

YOUR VALUES DETERMINE YOUR GOALS

Our society is a goal-oriented one. We cherish the idea of setting and achieving goals, and so we make goals and objectives the centerpiece of our manifestation intention. We have goals to acquire a big house, make a million dollars, and drive a fine car. But we are blind to the truth that while goals are important, they are subservient to our values. Your values will determine your goals, not the other way around. If one of your core values is simplicity and healthy living, then one of your goals when you try to manifest a new home will be a home with open land so that you can plant and harvest a rich garden of your own foods. If one of your core values is family, then you may instead try to attract a house with a separate wing for your aging parents, because having them close is in line with your value system.

There's that word again: *system*. I have spoken much of God's economic system on a grand cosmic scale, but the fact is that you, as a proxy for God, have a microcosm of that system in your Spirit: your values. That system moves every transaction in your life:

---

1. http://thinkexist.com/quotation/dont_let_special_characters_and_values-the/222988.html (accessed October 2009).

who you marry, what you do, how you vote, who your friends are, what you defend, what you buy. It determines the goals you pursue. Having manifestation goals that are not linked to your values—or even purely material goals, for that matter—will create dissonance and internal conflict in your Mind that will create misery and horror for you. This is why people trapped in the wrong careers are so desperate to get out; they are living the nightmare of defying their values.

GOD IS ALL VALUES

In a way, God is beyond the human conception of values. But since God is consciousness and ultimately the Alpha and Omega of all things, it only makes sense that he would not only possess all values simultaneously but be the very embodiment of them. That includes the negative values: greed, envy, control, and so on. God must embody every value that human beings can manifest, which is why it is absurd to characterize God as some sort of perfect, emotionless being. God is Consciousness. He is hate and love and sloth and courage and honor and every other state of being all at the same time. This is why he understands how we are driven and sometimes misguided by our values. He is their Source.

VALUES DO NOT CHANGE

What was honorable five thousand years ago in the deserts of the Sinai is probably still honorable today, and what was criminal is most likely still criminal. The spiritual concepts behind values are as close to eternal as anything human ever can be; as I said, they are absolutes in a relative plane of existence. Circumstances change, surroundings change, and culture changes, but values remain consistent. This is why they act as a North Star for us over the years, allowing us to look back at the patterns of behavior of others and to become wiser.

The persistence of values has another important effect on human evolution: it allows us to remain confident that the central principles to which we hitch our wagons today as we manifest the things and people of our futures will still be inspirational and God-like tomorrow. We do not have to worry about values going out of style like fashions or technology. They are eternal. Yes, some values do become dusty and ill-used in our modern age. Chastity has become something of a relic, but that does not mean it is not still practiced nor that it is not important. The ways in which we express our values have certainly altered with time; our system of dispensing justice has become more humane and wiser over the years. But the fundamental concept of justice has not changed by an atom since it was created at the dawn of Time.

Values give us the comfort of knowing that there is a consistent measure against which we can assess the progress of our character and ourselves in the eyes of God.

THE VALUES THAT INSPIRE

In our modern world, where so many grasp at the material and cling to credit and debt like drowning swimmers trying to escape a sinking ship, I have no doubt that the values of honor, honesty, and generosity have the most power to inspire. They do so because we live in an era when many people are encouraged to pursue fame for its own sake and do whatever they must for easy money. These actions encourage false identities, self-deception, and the betrayal of other values, such as thrift and fidelity, which are sacrificed on the altar of fame and influence. In such a world, many people feel that others cannot be trusted—that no one can ever be trusted. To come into this cesspit of deceit with an open heart and hand and exhibit pure honor (always keeping your word), honesty (always telling the truth), and generosity (giving others what they need even if you go without) can shock others. They simply don't expect those virtues. But that power can inspire with an electricity greater than that of any words.

You may find that other values inspire more effectively in your world, such as compassion or gratitude. You cannot go wrong when your values move others to question their own and discover the inner Spirit that creates those values. In any case, a small but mighty heartwood of values forms the center of all that we try to accomplish in manifestation and in moving others to follow our example. We are not the answer, but the question: "Why does that person have so much wealth and so much joy?" Our lives lead to the One Answer.

We have shared a great journey through the Laws of Prosperity, and I think it only fitting that it concludes with values. What this journey should reveal to you is that, despite the harrowing economic times in which we find ourselves, money is not the answer. It is the result of asking the correct questions and seeking the answers with a true heart, humility before God, and the awareness of the Truth: that you are a co-Creator with God, destined to serve his great purpose and to help him evolve as you evolve. Your values are the lever with which you can move the earth, but they are only one of twenty tools you have learned about in this book. Now that you possess them, go forth with the understanding that it is not what you do but who you are becoming that drives your future prosperity, enables you to overcome any temporary setbacks you are experiencing, and transforms you into someone who inspires others to greatness.

WHAT WE HAVE LEARNED

- Your values are your sliver of God's conscience.

- Values are your spirit speaking to your material Mind.

- Values, not actions, inspire others to enlightenment.

- Values do not change; you change.

CLOSING NOTE

■ ■ ■ ■ ■

There is no part of this book, not one of the Laws, that is less or more important than any other. The whole is the lesson. The entire landscape of prosperity is here ready to yield to your knowledge. God greatly desires your stewardship of his mission and purpose, and he wishes great wealth for you in order to make you able to exert the influence in the world that you must in order to do his will. It is your great destiny to be rich beyond measure in money, property, love, purpose, creativity, health, or all of the above. It is your birthright. Claim it. And when you have questions or wish to add insights to what I have written here, please share them with me at www.thelawsofprosperity.com. May God bless you and bring you abundance.

INDEX

■ ■ ■ ■ ■

INDEX

INDEX

INDEX

INDEX

INDEX

SUPPORTERS FOR THE
LAWS OF PROSPERITY

▪ ▪ ▪ ▪ ▪

I want to give a special acknowledgment to the following people for giving me the inspiration to write this book.

Rosonya Adil
Yutosha Alston
Brenda Armstead
Nichelle Austin
Fatima Duarte Bae
Bertha Bain
Anthony Bell
Kimberly Blake
Elizabeth Bobbitt
Patricia Boone
Ralph & Gloria Boyce
Angela Brown
Luvenia Bryant
Patricia Burns
Ionie Caldwell
Jeremiah Campbell
Hazel Claiborne
Cynthia Clark
Fred Clark
Mascareen Cohen

Patricia Colbert
Marchell Coleman
Jeanette Cox
Cynthia Davis
Nancy Dandy
Gurmay Darlington
Winston Davis, Jr.
Sandra Elder
Josephine Finn
Cheryl Frain
Alvin Freeman
Marcus & Barbara Fugate
Billy Gaines
Urban Garrett, Sr.
Darlene Graham
Denise Graham
Joyce Gardner
Gail George
James Glenn
Alva Gooden

Margaret Grant
Andrea Graves
Lisa Harrigan
Beatrice Hollins Hardy
Ottie Hill
Angela Horn
Kathy Hughes
Alice Jackson
Glorya Johnson
Iris Jones
Ophelia Hayes Jones
Debra Ann Jordan
Mary Jordan
Sheffian Joseph
Donald Kelley
Gloria Jean Kelley
Joan Lambert
Nellie Lane
Rose Leclaire
Marcus Legall
Mary Anne Lombardi
Darvi Mack
Jennaya Macklin
Annette Mckinney
Douglas Miller
Myra Moore
Edna Morgan
Kimberlee Morgan
Robin Morgan
Cyrilene Moulton
Lillian Murphy
Elisha Perry
Jerome Pillow
Douglas Ping
Omar Plummer
Tawanna Polk
Grace Pounder

Theresa Powell
Charese Preston
Willie Lee Pryor Sr.
Gregory Puga
Millicent Raglan
Barbara Reed
Heidi Rees
Anthony Reid
Cecilia Reid
Melanie Richards
Michael Richardson
Cheryl Riddick
Yolanda Rojas
Charisse Sanders
Immy Schollaardt
Cynthia Scott
Lillian Sergenton
Delmus Simmons
Patricia Skeete
Sharon Small
Ronald Smalls
Florence F. Smith
Theoma Southwell
Michelle Starr
Marcella Sullivan
Darnell Syphrett
Wesen Tekeste
Suzanne Thomas
Wynette Thomas
Portia Vaughn
Joyce Watkins
Leotorah Watson
Valerie Williams
Cynthia Wilson
Ellen Woods
Zoe Ministries International-Canada